Cambridge Elements

Elements in the Philosophy of Immanuel Kant
edited by
Desmond Hogan
Princeton University
Howard Williams
University of Cardiff
Allen Wood
Indiana University

KANT ON PROPERTY RIGHTS AND INTERNATIONAL LAW

Alice Pinheiro Walla
McMaster University

Shaftesbury Road, Cambridge CB2 8EA, United Kingdom

One Liberty Plaza, 20th Floor, New York, NY 10006, USA

477 Williamstown Road, Port Melbourne, VIC 3207, Australia

314–321, 3rd Floor, Plot 3, Splendor Forum, Jasola District Centre, New Delhi – 110025, India

103 Penang Road, #05–06/07, Visioncrest Commercial, Singapore 238467

Cambridge University Press is part of Cambridge University Press & Assessment, a department of the University of Cambridge.

We share the University's mission to contribute to society through the pursuit of education, learning and research at the highest international levels of excellence.

www.cambridge.org
Information on this title: www.cambridge.org/9781009644266

DOI: 10.1017/9781009402552

© Alice Pinheiro Walla 2026

This publication is in copyright. Subject to statutory exception and to the provisions of relevant collective licensing agreements, no reproduction of any part may take place without the written permission of Cambridge University Press & Assessment.

When citing this work, please include a reference to the DOI 10.1017/9781009402552

First published 2026

A catalogue record for this publication is available from the British Library

ISBN 978-1-009-64426-6 Hardback
ISBN 978-1-009-40258-3 Paperback
ISSN 2397-9461 (online)
ISSN 2514-3824 (print)

Cambridge University Press & Assessment has no responsibility for the persistence or accuracy of URLs for external or third-party internet websites referred to in this publication and does not guarantee that any content on such websites is, or will remain, accurate or appropriate.

For EU product safety concerns, contact us at Calle de José Abascal, 56, 1°, 28003 Madrid, Spain, or email eugpsr@cambridge.org

Kant on Property Rights and International Law

Elements in the Philosophy of Immanuel Kant

DOI: 10.1017/9781009402552
First published online: January 2026

Alice Pinheiro Walla
McMaster University

Author for correspondence: Alice Pinheiro Walla, pinheiro@mcmaster.ca

Abstract: This Element argues that property rights and the territorial rights of states in Kant's legal theory provide a strong justification for the expansion of international law. Central to the argument is Kant's theory of legal obligation, according to which a right to external things is only possible if it can genuinely bind all those on whom it must impose an external duty. Given the global scope of this legal obligation in Kant's account, it can only be achieved through the implementation of a shared international legal order regulated by a principle of reciprocity in external relations. Kant's conception of legal obligation thus requires us to leave the state of nature beyond domestic legal systems towards an international legal order. The author also examines how the international legal order differs from a world state, and how it can be consistent with national legal systems.

Keywords: Immanuel Kant, property rights, international law, territorial rights, legal obligation

© Alice Pinheiro Walla 2026

ISBNs: 9781009644266 (HB), 9781009402583 (PB), 9781009402552 (OC)
ISSNs: 2397-9461 (online), 2514-3824 (print)

Contents

1 Introduction: Skepticism about Property Rights   1

2 Kant's Theory of Possession   9

3 Kant's Theory of Acquisition and Common Possession of the Earth   18

4 International Law and *Rechtsstaatlichkeit*   29

5 What Is an International Civil Condition?   33

6 What Kant Does Differently   47

7 Kant's Non-Reductive Legal Positivism: Two Concepts of Right   51

8 Conclusion   63

List of Abbreviations   65

References   66

1 Introduction: Skepticism about Property Rights

In this Element, I argue that Kant's theory of legal obligation provides a distinctive argument for expanding and consolidating international law.[1] More specifically, a shared international legal order is required for the possibility of the legal obligation to respect property rights and the territorial rights of states everywhere.[2] Although the interpretation of some of the main tenets of Kant's legal theory and their implications remains a matter of ongoing debate in Kant scholarship, the argument I will present here is supported by textual evidence and a close charitable reading of Kant's legal philosophy. This is the case even when my analysis may lead to conclusions that expand Kant's legal theory beyond its original concerns and scope of application. The present work remains committed to what I take to be essential to Kant's legal thought and combines Kant scholarship and *applied* Kant scholarship to formulate a Kantian argument for international law.

An important warning at this point is that the concept "property rights" should not be conflated with *private* property rights (Macpherson 1978). Whether individual, collective or public, all forms of ownership ultimately presuppose the *authority* of right holders to decide, within reasonable constraints,[3] how the resource in question should be used against the competing claims and differing conceptions of others. This is true even of Indigenous groups who arguably conceive their relation to their native land as being radically different from Western conceptions of ownership, and may even deny that land is something that can be owned as property.[4] Also, these Indigenous groups require a prerogative to decide and bind outsiders as to how to relate with a specific area on planet earth that goes beyond merely empirically holding the land (see Rühl 2010, p. 570). Despite their distinctive ontology of land, or perhaps precisely *because* they hold a distinctive conception of how to relate to land compared to our Western understanding, Indigenous

---

[1] An earlier version of the arguments developed in this Cambridge Element was published as Pinheiro Walla (2024).
[2] Note that this is not an argument for a *world state*, but for an international *legal order*. I will say more about this in Sections 3.2, 4, and 5.
[3] I will leave the idea of "reasonable constraints" on the prerogatives of property holders deliberately open and vague. While one can conceive such constraints from a "natural law" perspective, with reference to a conception of the rationale or purpose of property rights, constraints on property rights may also be specified by statutory law. For instance, one may not use one's property to hurt or harm others. In any case, property rights are not absolute rights.
[4] In its early years, the indigenous rights discourse conceptualized Indigenous peoples' rights to lands and natural resources mainly as *cultural rights*. It allowed Indigenous peoples to hold land as required for their cultural rights, but excluded them from property rights on the basis of their specific ontology of land. Recently, indigenous rights to land are being increasingly reframed as property rights to land and resources. See Åhrén 2016, chapter 5, section 5.5.2, and chapter 8.

groups must be able to impose an *obligation* on outsiders to respect their distinctive relationship to land. Indeed, the greatest threat to Indigenous groups' physical and cultural integrity lies in the fact that they lack effective rights to determine how to live on their traditional territories (Kennedy et al. 2023). Therefore, pluralism about property and territory, that is, the possibility of different coexisting conceptions about how to relate with land and resources, cannot dispense with the idea of property rights as the legal power to decide and bind others in regard to external objects, including land, which Kant conceived of as *intelligibler Besitz,* intelligible possession or noumenal possession (*possessio noumenon*).[5] To give up the idea of property rights in general would be to give up the very possibility of *choosing* how to relate with the earth, its resources, and other persons, whether individually or collectively.

Kant's theory of property rights is therefore not about defending any substantive conception of property, but primarily about examining the conditions under which it is possible to think about the *authority* of right holders to bind all others to respect the way they choose to relate with their land and resources. As this Element will explain, while the fundamental concept of Kant's legal theory is *external freedom*, at the very heart of Kant's theory of property is a *theory of legal obligation* that motivates the whole architecture of Kant's legal thought. As we will see, Kant's initial aim in his theory of "rights to external things" is primarily analytical; his main concern is to provide an account of what he calls "merely rightful possession", that is, the concept of the normative conditions for the power to impose an external duty on all other persons generally. The upshot is that rights to land necessarily have a *global* dimension that inevitably leads us to think about international law. Because territorial rights and rights to external things are being considered from the perspective of the possibility of legal obligation, it is possible to think about territorial rights to a certain extent analogously to property rights, without the contentious implication that territorial rights must be understood as the "private property" of their people.[6]

Kant's theory of property rights establishes a framework for property rights within a specific, geographically determined legal order. However, an important

---

[5] MS 6: 245 and 249. Not to be confused with *intellectual* property rights.
[6] In contrast to other rightful relations that involve only the choices of the parties, both property rights and territorial rights involve claims to external things. They also require the possibility of original acquisition (Section 3). The analogy between property rights and territorial rights, however, has limits. Territorial rights presuppose both the idea of the civil union of individuals into a people (understood as a juridical-political collective), and of their political representation by the state. Therefore, states' jurisdiction over a territory is defined by its representative function and the purpose of the civil union; further, territorial rights incorporate and do not abolish individuals' and groups' titles to specific parts of the land. Since a territory-based legal order is necessary for property rights internally, we can conclude that property rights are normatively prior to (or more fundamental) than territorial rights, although historically this may not be the case.

implication of Kant's theory of property is that right not only can, but should be extended to an international legal framework, for reasons that I reconstruct and elucidate in the course of my exposition. However, as Kant acknowledges, the international expansion of legal frameworks is not without problems and concerns that it could lead to hegemony and tyranny between states. Kant scholars also disagree about what is Kant's own position in light of these concerns and the seemingly contradictory statements in the relevant passages on the law of nations (see Kleingeld 2004, 2012). While my inquiry could be restricted to addressing objections arising from within Kant's own theoretical framework, I will preamble the actual task of this Element with a brief discussion of more general objections and grounds for skepticism directed to the main themes of the Element. One relates to the idea of international law itself, which is often considered problematic or "no real law" (see, e.g., Hart 2012 / 1961). The other regards the much-vilified idea of property rights itself, often derided as a mere tool for domination and exploitation. Hostility to the idea of property rights tends to be associated in the public discourse and imagination with Marx's critique of property, but erroneously so.[7] Another concern is that even if one were to recognize the right to property domestically, one may nevertheless reject the idea of an *international* system of property rights. Traditionally, property law was regarded as a domestic concern (Sprankling 2012). If property rights are already protected domestically, international property law may arouse the suspicion that it is a mere pretext for powerful investors to undermine state regulations, as opposed to preventing states from abusing power (Been and Beauvais 2003). Finally, one could object that an international property rights system would necessitate the *homogenization* of domestic property systems, eroding the plurality of property conceptions, and the sovereignty of states (Dagan 2021). These concerns may explain the relatively sparse literature on property rights and international law, in contrast to, for instance, the vast literature on property rights and economic development.

According to the view that property rights in general are illegitimate, property rights are coercive instruments aimed at protecting the interests of the dominant social classes to the detriment of the genuine and more basic needs of humanity as a whole. Because property rights are regarded as the defining feature of capitalism, the rejection of property rights in general is usually associated with a critique of capitalism. The capitalist conception of property distorts the real needs of human beings and alienates them from these needs.[8] It

---

[7] See footnote 11.
[8] This view tends to be associated with Marx, given his critique of alienation within the capitalist system. However, according to Marx himself, the distinguishing feature of communism is not the abolition of property altogether, but only of *bourgeois* property (Marx and Engels 1963 / 1848).

forces those who lack property in the means of production to lose control over the definition of their own needs and serve alien purposes. The focus on the protection of property rights would also incentivize the suspension of political rights and freedoms and consequently erode democracy.

Underlying this view is (i) the idea that exclusion is the defining feature of property rights in general and (ii) a conflation of the concept of property rights with private property and capitalism. Consequently, the proper antidote to exclusion and exploitation is the abolition of the institution of property and of the capitalist system. While it is not the aim of this Element to provide a justification or defense of capitalism, it is worth stressing that a critical stance or even the rejection of capitalism altogether does not eliminate the need to theorize about property rights. Implicit in the idea of alienation as social critique is the idea that there must be a correct or at least alternative way to conceptualize the relationship between labor and external resources, and the relations of persons towards each other in regard to external resources. The idea of a rights violation against the workers, as well as the authority to bind (which is tacitly assumed as void in the case of the capitalist) presupposes a conception of ideal property relations. That is the case even if a substantive conception of property relations, namely that characteristic of the capitalist system, is being rejected. Without an analytic theory of property rights one can merely presuppose but not adequately conceptualize the idea of a property rights violation when it comes to exploited and dispossessed groups. Neither can one account theoretically for alternative ways of interacting with the earth and its resources in a way that would not involve arbitrarily imposing one's own conception of property on another person or group, thereby replicating the domination one is so eager to reject. Sincerely believing in the moral correctness of one's views does not render its external imposition on others less arbitrary.

As we will see, property rights from a Kantian perspective are fundamentally *relational* rights, that is, entitlements persons hold against each other. This is a feature of *all* property relations, not only of private property as a specific form of property relations. As long as the authority to determine how property is to be used is held *against another person or all other persons*, abolishing private property or changing the form of property arrangements would merely amount to *transferring* the authority to decide in regard to external possessions away from individuals or groups to a larger collective or different group. This would not amount to the abolition of property rights altogether, but merely of a specific form of property relations. In contrast, this Element suggests that Kant's legal theory can help us achieve a better understanding of the structure of rights relations in regard to external things, which allows us to think more clearly about property rights.

It can also be argued that a well-functioning and inclusive property rights system is crucial for securing and protecting the rights of the poor and of vulnerable groups, who are often excluded from the formal property rights system. This includes traditional ownership, such as Indigenous peoples' rights to their ancestral lands, and the land tenure and homes of long-standing communities. Advocates of international property rights view the right to property as a human right that needs international implementation and further development. Other arguments in favor of international property rights highlight the economic benefits of formal property rights for the poor and marginalized groups, and the possibility of restitution or compensation in case of expropriation worldwide.

Although violations of the property rights of vulnerable and marginalized groups are a global problem, property rights insecurity is neglected in discussions of rights violations of vulnerable groups (Lawson-Remer 2012). The underlying assumption seems to be that vulnerable groups do not hold property at all, or that protecting property rights would *prevent* redistribution in their favor. Both assumptions are misconceptions. Poor persons often possess significant assets such as plots of land, produce, a home, and small businesses. However, a common problem faced by vulnerable populations around the globe is that they very often lack a *formal title* to their possessions. Kant himself does not rule out state taxation and redistribution as being incompatible with property rights: he defends the state right to tax the rich and redistribute to maintain the poor in society as based on the duty of the rich towards the state for the protection of their property (MS 6: 325–6 and MS 6: 454).[9] Property rights are not absolute rights: they may be limited by law or even superseded by other rights and considerations, such as reasons of state or the public good.

An objection could be that by giving the poor access to capital this proposal would promote capitalism. However, the formalization of property for these communities could help lift millions of persons out of poverty, while leaving it to the communities themselves to manage their own assets, as they had informally done before. A strong and *inclusive* property system could thus create economic opportunities for the poor (de Soto 2000, chapter 3). According to this view, it is therefore the *inequality in access* to formal property rights and legal services that allows the privileged few to exploit and benefit disproportionately from the property system. A well-functioning and inclusive property rights system is a crucial mechanism for securing and protecting the rights of the poor and of vulnerable groups, who are excluded from the formal property rights system.

---

[9] For discussion, see Baiasu (2014), Holtman (2018), Pinheiro Walla (2019), and Loriaux (2020).

Where persons have no formal title to their land and resources and can be arbitrarily dispossessed, authoritarian governments exploit natural resources with no accountability or concern for redistribution to the citizens. Implementing legal mechanisms at the international level, formalizing titles domestically and strengthening the property rights of private persons and communities could help mitigate the resource curse by offering vulnerable groups legal recourse against dispossession for the exploitation of natural resources. Therefore, property rights can also protect vulnerable populations against undue state interference and expropriation (Kriebaum & Reinisch 2019).

The views I have sketched illustrate the way secure property rights and the rule of law can contribute to economic development as well as provide protection against arbitrary dispossession and exploitation from domestic governments and international actors. From a Kantian perspective, these are *instrumental* arguments for a system of property rights: They constitute a means to an end.

Kant's account is distinctive because it offers a *noninstrumental* argument for property rights. While it is compatible with and can lend support to economic development views, Kant's theory regards the implementation of an international property rights system as a requirement for the *bindingness* of property rights, that is, for the legal obligation that corresponds to a right *in rem*.

Characteristic of a right *in rem* or multital right or claim is that it resides in a single person (or specific group of persons) but holds against other persons as a "very large and indefinite class of people" (Hohfeld 1917). Spelling out the normative conditions for the possibility of a multital right is one of the fundamental tasks of Kant's legal theory. International law turns out to be important for the possibility of multital rights in general. The argument also extends to the territorial rights of states. However, this is not because Kant erroneously treats national territory as the "private property of states," but because territory also requires imposing external obligations on outsiders, thereby raising the same difficulties in regard to the possibility of legal obligation as property rights. "External" or "legal obligations" (I will use the terms interchangeably) designate duties that can be externally *coerced*. Given the element of coercion bound up with legal duties (in Kant's terminology, *Rechtspflichten* or "duties of right"), external duties require a distinctive theory of obligation for their legitimacy that is not exhausted by ethical considerations.[10]

---

[10] It is important to note that Kant distinguished between Morals (*Sitten*) and Ethics (*Ethik*, also identified with *Tugend*, virtue, and *Tugendpflichten*, duties of virtue). Both *Recht* (translated as "Right" or "Law") and *Ethik* are subsumed under the wider category of *Sitten* understood as Morals in general, that is, the area of philosophy concerned with the laws of *freedom* as opposed

Because the main task of Kant's theory of property rights is to spell out the formal conditions under which rights to things external to us can impose corresponding duties on others, and not to prescribe any specific property rights arrangement, it is compatible with pluralism about property relations, within certain normative constraints.[11] It does not commit us to adopt a homogeneous view of property relations which ignores or seeks to eradicate domestic differences. The concrete configuration of property relations is secondary and understood as "derived" from the collective will of individual right holders. It is an empirical aspect that results from the choice of a collective. Fundamental to the Kantian conception of property is the requirement that possessors and nonpossessors alike must be symmetrically situated under a public legal order with the authority to adjudicate in case of rights disputes because only under such an arrangement are our external relations structured in such a way that *it is permissible* to coerce. Although it is possible to conceive persons as "coercing each other" under such reciprocity relations, reciprocity of coercion is in fact only possible if no private persons are unilaterally coercing another, but coercion comes from a public authority that represents and therefore binds all private persons *equally*. Note that this is a *formal* argument about the structure of external relations between persons, not a (trivial) claim about the need for coercive institutions to protect and enforce rights. This formal requirement acquires a global dimension once we consider that different national systems also stand in external relations to each other that require such a formal structure. A certain degree of centralization and coordination of a plurality of domestic legal systems, rather than the imposition of a specific configuration of property relations "from above" is thus the task prescribed by a Kantian conception of international property rights.

1.1 The Structure of the Element

Kant's overall argument in his theory of property rights follows three main steps. The first step culminates in the conclusion that being able to use external objects of choice is constitutive of external freedom; ruling out the notion of a *rightful possession* of objects of choice would amount to denying ourselves

---

to the laws of nature or causal determinism. However, Kant differentiates between Right and Ethics as based on two distinctive forms of legislation (*Gesetzgebung*), directed at external and internal freedom respectively. Therefore, Morals (*Sitten*) should not be conflated with Ethics or Virtue. See MS 6: 219–220.

[11] Pluralism about property is the view that there is no single way to define or distribute property. Kant does not prescribe a private property-based system. However, given the rational principles regulating rightful relations and the Kantian state, Kant's legal theory recognizes normative constraints on what can count as a *rightful* system of property. Kant's position is thus pluralism within certain constraints. I would like to thank an anonymous referee for stressing this point.

a fundamental aspect of external freedom, and would lead to a contradiction of reason with itself. I will reconstruct and elucidate Kant's argument for intelligible possession (*intelligibler Besitz, possessio noumenon*) in Section 2 ("Kant's Theory of Possession").

The second step of Kant's argument involves the view that acquisition of external objects must be conceptualized as unilateral acts of appropriation that nevertheless require ex-ante a form of legal community. Natural law thinkers before Kant appealed to the notion of common possession of the earth to account for this prepositive legal community, which they conceived as a primordial communism of land and resources: because the earth was given to us in common by the Creator, it must be permissible for individuals to unilaterally separate and use the earth's resources for the satisfaction of their needs. I argue in Section 3 ("Kant's Theory of Acquisition and Common Possession of the Earth") that Kant offers a unique account of the community of the earth that is compatible with his critical thought, and radically redefines (i.e., "Kantianizes") the conceptual framework he takes over from the natural law tradition.

The third and final step of Kant's argument is the most important for the purposes of this Element. Kant spells out the normative conditions for a right in external objects, including possession of land, to impose an obligation on all others (Section 3.2). Although the right to use objects and occupy land is based on the Kantian equivalent of natural law (i.e., *Vernunftrecht* or "Right of Reason"), Kant puts forward a version of legal positivism that is motivated by nonpositive concerns. Rights to external things and land ultimately necessitate public systems of law, not for mere prudential reasons (to "protect" property rights), but as a formal requirement for the possibility of legal obligation. Because Kant recognizes that property rights and territorial rights impose duties that are *global in scope*, they call for the implementation of an international law system. It follows that public law systems cannot be confined to the domestic level (Section 4, "International Law and *Rechtsstaatlichkeit*"). However, Kant was also aware of the dangers associated with giving international law coercive powers and with implementation challenges. I therefore discuss the conditions potential member states in international law must satisfy lest international law be instrumentalized for the private interests and agendas of despots, as opposed to promoting the international rule of law and peace.

Sections 5, 6, and 7 further develop specific aspects of the overall argument of this Element. Section 5 ("What is an International Civil Condition?") examines the question of how to understand the hierarchy between domestic and international legal orders. For this, I draw upon Kelsen's idea of the unity of legal cognition and his views on international law in order to elucidate Kant's position. Section 6 ("What Kant Does Differently") reflects upon the distinctive contribution of Kant's theory to theorizing about property rights and law in general, and compares them with his predecessors John Locke and Jean-Jacques Rousseau. Since one of the views I defend in the Element is that Kant is a legal positivist, Section 7 analyzes the uniqueness of Kant's legal positivism, and criticizes two interpretations of Kant's legal theory as non-positivist. The conclusion summarizes the argument of the Element.

2 Kant's Theory of Possession

In this section, I will reconstruct the first step in Kant's argument for an international system of property rights, namely his account of possession of external objects in general. But before we start, I will briefly summarize the main tenets of Kant's legal theory in general, and explain how his theory of possession of external objects is embedded within this broader theoretical framework.

Kant's legal theory is based on the idea of a *system* of external freedom, that is, the view that the external relations between a pluralities of persons should be regulated and coordinated by a rational principle that ensures reciprocity and therefore excludes arbitrary coercion of one person over another. This fundamental principle is the so-called Universal Principle of Right (MS 6: 230–1):

> Any action is right if it can coexist with everyone's freedom in accordance with a universal law, or if on its maxim the freedom of choice of each can coexist with everyone's freedom in accordance with a universal law. (MS 6: 230)

But what does a universal law mean in this context? Universality in Kant's theory is nothing other than the insight that *rational necessity formally translates into reciprocity*. Universality has long been misunderstood as the expectation that a rational principle (such as the Categorical Imperative of Kant's ethical theory) will be applicable to all agents regardless of the circumstances and yield the same conclusions across a variety of scenarios. As numerous attempts to debunk the Categorical Imperative test by showing how it leads to absurd results suggest, universality understood in that way misses the point. Instead, Kant has in mind the idea that rational principles are universal because they express something fundamental about our rational nature. These fundamental principles are *binding* for each and every agent as a matter of *rational consistency*. This shared "ground of obligation" anchored in our rational nature and constitutive of our "personality" is what will lead us to the requirement to *respect* all other persons while at the same time *claiming respect* from them.

Rationality in Kant's philosophy is thus intrinsically connected to the view that universality amounts to reciprocity.

Another fundamental tenet of Kant's theory is the radically equal status of each and every person. Reciprocity affirms this radical equality. Applied to *external* freedom, reciprocity means reconciling the capacity of choice of every agent with that of others. Whatever the substantive content of their particular choices, external relations between persons must be formally compatible with the equal status of each individual; their spheres of external freedom must be equally affirmed. This requirement of reciprocity is clearly stated in Kant's definition of the only innate right and the related concept of the *innate equality* between persons, that is, "independence from being bound by others to more than one can in turn (*wechselseitig*) bind them" (MS 6: 237). Rights to objects outside our own bodies are relevant to the exercise of external freedom insofar as they are *objects of choice* (*Willkür*) (MS 6: 246).[12] But since all rights must be understood as relations between *persons*, rights to external objects must also have the form of reciprocity in order to be binding. Kant's theory of possession must thus explain how external objects can become the possession of someone, and under which conditions possession of a thing can constitute a right.

Central for Kant's theory of possession is Kant's distinction between *empirical possession* and *intelligible possession*. The distinction is based on the insight that a right to an external object presupposes the possibility of being *wronged* in one's right. However, reducing possession to a mere *empirical* connection to an object would necessarily undermine the possibility of identifying a wrong. There would be no conceptual way to differentiate between a violation of one's physical integrity when the object is snatched away from your hands and a rightful claim to that thing. A rightful claim must hold even when one is not physically connected to the object. For instance, my coat is mine even if I am not wearing it right now and someone else is wearing it instead. It follows that a right to a thing requires thinking about possession in a purely *juridical* manner; it must be conceived as going beyond mere physical connection to an object. It also requires understanding rights to external objects primarily as a relation between persons in regard to an object, and not directly as a relation between a person and a thing. Hence Kant's criticism of Locke's "guardian spirit" theory of property (Ripstein 2009, p. 22).

---

[12] See also Kant's mature distinction between *Wille* and *Willkür*, which tracks the distinction between internal and external freedom (MS 6: 213).

2.1 Two Concepts of Possession

Kant does not take for granted the view that there are such things as rights to external objects. While he postulates an innate right to be free from arbitrary interference on our immediate external actions and physical integrity (MS 6: 237–8), this innate right does not include rights to external things outside one's own body. Therefore, the inclusion of external objects within the scope of external freedom requires an additional argument. Kant thus proceeds to offer a formal argument why we must assume the possibility of rights to external objects, beyond the scope of innate right. His starting point is a conceptual truth: having a right in an external object means that anyone interfering with that object without the right holder's consent is committing a *wrong* (*Läsion*):

> That is *rightfully* mine (*meum iuris*) with which I am so connected that another's use of it without my consent would wrong me. The subjective condition of any possible use is *possession*. But something *external* would be mine only if I may assume that I could be wronged by another's use of a thing even *though I am not in possession of it*. – So it would be self-contradictory to say that I have something external as my own if the concept of possession could not have different meanings, namely *sensible* possession and *intelligible* possession, and by the former could be understood *physical* possession but by the latter a *merely rightful* possession of the same object. (MS 6: 245)

Having a right to an external object, that is, something that can exist in a different location from me, conceptually entails the possibility of being wronged by another's interference with that object without my consent. If it is possible to be wronged by another's interference even if one is not physically connected to the object in question, we must assume a conceptual distinction between physically holding an object (*Inhabung, detentio*) and possessing an object in a "merely rightful" sense (*bloß rechtlich besitzen*). What is new is the idea of possessing something "merely rightfully." The concept of possessing an object "merely rightfully" requires us to think about possession of objects independently of whether one is currently physically connected with that object. Otherwise, the concept of arbitrary interference would apply only to interference with one's bodily integrity while holding the object. We would not be able to conceptualize a violation of a right to an external object per se. For this, we must understand the wrong in question as an interference with the right holder's *authority* to dispose of her object as she sees fit, independently of its physical location and who is empirically holding it. The concept of a right to something in general must be thus conceived as a metaphysical category, namely, as *intelligible* possession (MS 6: 245–6):

> [...] right is a pure practical *rational concept* of choice under laws of freedom.
>
> For the same reason it is not appropriate to speak of possessing a right to this or that object but rather of possessing it *merely rightfully* [*bloß rechtlich besitzen*]; for a right is already an intellectual possession of an object and it would make no sense to speak of possessing a possession. (MS 6: 249)

But what *entitles* us to assume "merely rightful possession" of an object? In Kant's words, "how is *merely rightful* (intelligible) possession possible?" "Possibility" in this case amounts to explaining why a "*synthetic* a priori proposition" about right is not a mere fiction (MS 6: 249).[13] While having something in my possession is analogous to an analytical truth (to hold your book in my hands right now is for me *to have* that book, in a tautological sense), the concept of merely rightful possession enables us to think about possession *beyond* an actual empirical connection with the object. Rightful possession is thus a *synthetic proposition* because it tells us more than what is given by the senses or by mere conceptual definition. It is only thanks to the metaphysical distinction between *empirical* and *intelligible* possession that we are able to understand that although I am holding this book, the book is nevertheless *yours*, as a matter of mere right. The "possibility" of this proposition, however, still needs to be demonstrated. Following the jurisprudence of his time, Kant calls the proof of the "title" of a concept a *deduction* (MS 6: 249–50).

2.2 The Deduction of the Concept of "Merely Rightful Possession"

The deduction of the concept of merely rightful possession proceeds by means of a purely formal, "apagogical" argument (MS 6: 246; Bucher 2007; Pinheiro Walla 2026). An apagogical argument is an indirect proof of a proposition (from the Greek *apagein*, "to lead away"). It asserts that it is necessary to assume or reject a certain proposition in order to preserve another proposition whose truth cannot be denied. Kant's argument is that merely rightful possession must be assumed to avoid a contradiction. The contradiction consists in affirming a proposition that would be incompatible with an end required by reason. Asserting the proposition that *it is not rightful to make use of an object of choice* would lead to a contradiction of practical reason with itself because it negates the idea, fundamental to practical rationality itself, that rational beings have the capacity to use external objects for exercising their freedom, that is, as *objects of choice*. Therefore, the requirement to avoid a contradiction of practical reason

---
[13] Cf. Kant's discussion of the possibility of the Categorical Imperative in the Third Section of the Groundwork (GMS 4: 453), and his mention of morality as being "no phantasm" (*eine chimärische Idee ohne Wahrheit*) in GMS 4: 445.

with itself rationally necessitates the *negation* of that proposition: it *must be rightful* to make use of objects of choice. Consequently, merely rightful possession must be possible. The contradiction arises because practical reason is bound to preserve its own functioning. Declaring potential objects of choice incapable of rightfully belonging to anyone would amount to rendering them "out of bounds" from a practical perspective (*res nullius*, "things belonging to no one"). Because practical deliberation is about the exercise of choice, reason would be negating its own foundations by *arbitrarily* choosing to deprive itself from its own power to use objects of choice. Declaring external objects *res nullius* would be an act of sheer *voluntarism*, not an expression of practical rationality.

> If it were nevertheless absolutely not within my *rightful* power to make use of it, that is, if the use of it could not coexist with the freedom of everyone in accordance with a universal law (would be wrong), then freedom would be depriving itself of the use of its choice with regard to an object of choice, by putting *usable* objects beyond any possibility of being *used*; in other words, it would annihilate them in a practical respect and make them into *res nullius*, even though in the use of things choice was formally consistent with everyone's outer freedom in accordance with universal laws. (MS 6: 250)

Kant concludes that postulating – that is, assuming for practical purposes – that we must treat objects of choice as the potential rightful possession of someone can also be called a "permissive law (*lex permissiva*) of practical reason" (MS 6: 247). As we will see in Section 2.3, the role of such a permissive law is to enable a specific legal position in the state of nature which could not otherwise be derived from "mere concepts of right" (MS 6: 247). This is the "moral capacity" of a rightful possessor to impose an obligation on all others to refrain from using that object without the rightful possessor's consent. The permissive law transforms the modality of unilateral acts of acquisition from *morally indifferent* into juridically significant deeds which can give rise to obligations (Hruschka 2004; Pinheiro Walla 2026).

In the first *Critique*, Kant warned against the use of apagogical arguments in metaphysics (A791–794/B819–822).[14] Transcendental proofs – that is, proofs that demonstrate the very possibility of knowledge, be it theoretical or practical – must never be apagogic but always *ostensive*. This means that it is not sufficient for philosophy to show that something is true in virtue of the logical elimination of contrary propositions; it must also account for *why* it is true (Guyer 2024, p. 23). Philosophy must thus provide insight into the

---

[14] I would like to thank an anonymous referee for the suggestion to address this issue.

transcendental conditions of the object of knowledge. If this is so, why is an apagogical proof appropriate in the case of merely rightful possession?

Apagogical proofs are necessary when no direct proof of a proposition is possible. For instance, Kant resorts to apagogical argumentation in his application of the first formulation of the Categorical Imperative in the *Groundwork* (GMS 4: 421). As a purely formal principle, the Categorical Imperative yields no substantive content until it is applied to a *maxim*, that is, a subjective principle of action, embedded in a concrete agent's situational context and motivational reality. When a maxim cannot be universalized – that is, is *impermissible* according to the formal standards expressed by the Categorical Imperative – a specific obligation is derived apagogically from the negation of the impermissible maxim. This particular obligation will be expressed either as a command to abstain from an action (a duty of *omission*) or to perform a specific action (a duty of *commission*). The substantive categorical imperative arising from the application of the formal Categorial Imperative to a specific maxim is thus an *apagogical conclusion*. As Bucher (2007, p. 998) observes, an apagogical argument is necessary in the case of the application of the Categorical Imperative because it is not possible to determine *directly* what is morally good; we can only define what is good by implication, with reference to what is morally bad or impermissible. What morality commands as one's duty (*Gebot*) is thus defined by what is ruled out by the moral principle (*Verbot*). This is what Kant means when he says that morality for us is expressed in the form of *duty* (*Pflicht*), as an action commanded as morally necessary from reverence to the moral principle (GMS 4: 400). We do not experience morality or our freedom directly, but always mediated through our awareness of *duty* (GMS 4: 457).

Merely rightful possession is *ideal*, that is, nonempirical possession. How can one prove that there is such a thing as a *title* to external things that is independent of an empirical connection with the object? Philosophy cannot provide a metaphysical (theoretical) proof of the existence of "intelligible possession" but only a *practical* argument why intelligible possession must be posited from the perspective of practical reason itself. Kant's apagogical argument relies on two contradictory premises (a *thesis* and an *antithesis*). Similarly to the need to check maxims against the Categorical Imperative, thesis and antithesis must be tested by the Universal Principle of Right, according to which

> any action is right if it can coexist with everyone's freedom in accordance with a universal law, or if on its maxim the freedom of choice of each can coexist with everyone's freedom in accordance with a universal law. (MS 6: 230)

The thesis affirms that intelligible possession is possible; the antithesis negates the possibility of intelligible possession, reducing all use of objects to mere empirical facts. The formal condition expressed by the Universal Principle of Right for the evaluation of each proposition is that a maxim must be able to coexist with everyone's freedom of choice in accordance with a universal law. In other words: at stake is the possibility of *coexistence of the choice of all* on the basis of that principle. As we saw, Kant argues that the antithesis would lead to things belonging to no one (*herrenlos, res nullius*, MS 6: 246), that is, it would not be possible to consider an external object as the belonging (*suum*) of someone, *as a matter of principle*. The implication would be that unless one is holding the object, one has no title to it. The antithesis thus embodies *realism about possession* (Rühl 2010, p. 570). Only the choice of those who happen to be in empirical possession is possible according to the antithesis. In the preparatory works to the Doctrine of Right, Kant illustrates the implications of the realist position about possession. Nobody's work would be safe from the infringement of others; it would not be against *Recht* to destroy what others have built or invested in (Vorarbeiten RL 23: 281). However, it is telling that Kant did not include this argumentation in the published version of the Doctrine of Right. Kant's point is not a concern about the empirical consequences of failing to recognize a nonempirical title to external things, although these would certainly be devastating for any form of long-term planning, industry or culture. Kant's point is a formal one. The antithesis asserts the *de iure* impossibility of rightful possession with the implication that genuine *choice* with regard to an external thing would be ruled out as a matter of conceptual truth. Although one could be lucky to control an object empirically and exclude others by force or cunning, one could not be said to dispose of the object as one sees fit. Choice evaporates since empirical possession is all or nothing control of things; a zero-sum game with no place for choice, let alone the choice of all. Choice over an external thing requires more than the contingency of empirical control; it requires *legal* power over an external thing, in relation to all others. The individual domain of authority over a thing is what formally enables choice. But since all rights are relational, legal power is by definition a capacity that must take into account the equal legal status of others, as a community of right holders. Unlike empirical possession, intelligible possession must be based on a principle expressing reciprocal relations: it must be compatible with a universal principle. A right is therefore a category that is only possible if it is genuinely universal in its foundations. Formally speaking, rights relations are never a zero-sum game. If I have the capacity to be the rightful possessor of a thing, so do you, as a matter of principle.

It follows that only the thesis is compatible with the Universal Principle of Right and preserves the fundamental assumption of Kant's theory of external freedom, namely, the possibility of the choice of a multitude of free and equal agents in accordance with a universal law.

2.3 Lex Permissiva

Distinctive of Kant's theory of obligation is that only an act of choice that has *universal* character – that is, is neither contingent nor unilateral – can be the basis for a "moral capacity" to obligate another. This "omnilaterality requirement" is also essential for the rightful use of external coercion, in contrast to mere arbitrary force. The problem is that while Kant acknowledges that such conditions of omnilaterality can only be achieved in the civil condition, acts of acquisition must take place already in the state of nature. A *lex permissiva* is thus needed to create possessors' moral capacity to bind prior to the institution of a positive legal order.

The prevailing interpretation among Kant scholars is that Kant introduces the notion of a *lex permissiva* as an authorization to something which would be otherwise morally contentious; in the case of rightful possession, its morally objectionable aspect would be the *exclusion* of others from the use of external things.[15] Call this the "exclusion view" of merely rightful possession. In contrast, Sharon Byrd and Joachim Hruschka argue that the role of the *lex permissiva* is to account for the *power* of right holders to impose an obligation on all others.[16] This obligation is correlative to the authority we must assume possessors have, given the concept of an object of choice, and not the attempt to "legitimize exclusion." Although the distinction between these two interpretations of *lex permissiva* may seem too subtle at first, regarding the permissive law as a power-conferring norm is central for understanding the place of Kant's theory of possession within his larger theory of legal obligation:

> This postulate can be called a permissive law (*lex permissiva*) of practical reason, which gives us an authorization that could not be got from mere concepts of right as such, namely to put all others under an obligation, which they would not otherwise have, to refrain from using certain objects of our choice because we have been the first to take them into our possession.

---

[15] Proponents of the prevailing reading of permissive laws as "justification for wrongdoing" are for instance Brandt (1982), Eberl and Niesen (2011), Horn (2014, p. 215), Tierney (2001a, 2001b), and Ypi (2014). For an excellent discussion and criticism of this reading, see Brecher (2026).

[16] Byrd and Hruschka (2010) argue that the prevailing reading applies only to the permissive laws in Perpetual Peace, and not to permissive laws in the Doctrine of Right (pp. 94–106). See also Hruschka (2004, 2015) and Ripstein (2009).

Reason wills that this hold as a principle, and it does this as *practical* reason, which extends itself a priori by this postulate of reason. (MS 6: 247)

Kant's concern is to explain how it is possible to put others under an obligation, *which they would not otherwise have*. The first question is: why would they not have that obligation without the *lex permissiva*? Although Kant's first argumentative step led us to assume the possibility of "merely rightful possession" of external objects, the formal conditions for the capacity of possessors to impose an external obligation on others are not yet in place. A further argument is needed. We must now consider the acts through which persons appropriate resources for themselves, that is, the normative status of *acquisition* of external objects. How can acquisition by an individual give rise to an obligation applying to all other persons to defer to her choice over an object? Kant's aim is not to suggest that there is something wrong about the choice of one person being able to exclude everybody else from a specific resource. As a matter of fact, exclusion is not even a necessary outcome of postulating rightful possession. A rightful possessor can choose to share their possession with others, or even to unite with other possessors to establish a communism of resources. Rightful possession is first and foremost about her authority to choose, not the content of her choices. Kant's main concern is to stress that if an agent is to have the authority to decide how to dispose of an object, her prerogative requires a jural relation to others that has a bearing on their external freedom. But that obligation cannot arise from the arbitrary, unilateral deed of an individual; it can only bind if it has a universal character and thus satisfies specific formal requirements.

As the next section will explain, the problem arises from the way *first* acquisition must be conceptualized, namely, as an individual act based on a "first come, first serve" principle of distribution. This aspect of first acquisition creates a problem for the obligation corresponding to merely rightful possession, given the way Kant understands the *structure* of obligation in general.

Acts of appropriation are unilateral: they are *contingent* in character and have per se no capacity to create obligations for other persons. From a Kantian perspective, legal obligation must have an *omnilateral* character in order to be genuinely binding. "Omnilaterality" in Kant's legal theory amounts to the *external version* of universality in Kant's ethics (Pinheiro Walla 2022, p. 111).

As stressed earlier, obligation within a Kantian conception must satisfy *formal conditions of reciprocity* in order to be valid; and reciprocity necessarily involves *universality*. This applies to both ethical and legal obligations, although the way Kant spells out reciprocity and universality is distinctive for each normative domain.

When it comes to *internal* freedom, we must be able to universalize our maxims; they must have the *form of a law* (GMS 4: 431). When thinking about *external* freedom, we must regulate our external relations with each other in accordance with external laws that formally establish reciprocity in these relations. This is not a mere application of ethical reasoning to our relations to other persons. As we will see, only shared *positive* legal orders can structure the external relations between persons in such a way as to establish omnilaterality.

The authorization introduced by the permissive law is necessary neither to "make wrongs right" nor to introduce an exception to a general moral rule. Instead, its role is to create a moral capacity that cannot be derived from mere concepts of rights alone.[17] Kant stresses that "*original* acquisition can be only *provisional. – Conclusive* acquisition takes place only in the civil condition" (MS 6: 264). As we will see in the next section, Kant's solution to the problem of legal obligation is to conceive unilateral acquisition as authorized ex ante by an originally constituted community of the earth ("provisional acquisition"), but conclusively binding only under a public system of laws ("conclusive acquisition"). This leads us to the postulate of public right (MS 6: 307), or the "Kantian *exeundum*," that is, the duty to leave the state of nature. In contrast to the Hobbesian and Lockean versions, the Kantian *exeundum* regards legal orders as necessary as a matter of *duty*, not out of prudential considerations or convenience.

3 Kant's Theory of Acquisition and Common Possession of the Earth

In this section, I reconstruct Kant's theory of acquisition and discuss how it leads to the duty to leave the state of nature and constitute a civil condition. Kant's theory of acquisition is the second step in his account of rights to external things. A theory of acquisition is required as Kant's second argumentative step because acquiring something external amounts to the application of the postulate that it must be possible to possess an external thing "merely rightfully." Although it is conceptually distinct from merely rightful possession, empirical possession is nevertheless the subjective condition for the *use* of external things. On the other hand, the *title* of possession is established through the rational idea of merely rightful possession (MS 6: 264). Acquisition has therefore two

---

[17] To our modern ears, the term "permissive" may suggest some form of license or an excuse not to follow a certain rule or principle. But it is possible to understand the permissibility in a different way. It is helpful to compare Kant's account of permissive laws to that of his predecessor Gottfried Achenwall. For Achenwall, permissive laws pertained to morally neutral matters, which were neither morally prescribed nor morally forbidden. See Achenwall (2020 / 1763), Introduction to Natural Law, II, §48.

dimensions: an *empirical* act of appropriation together with a *rational* title to possess that has normative implications for the rights and duties of others. Although they are bundled together in the concept of acquisition, these two dimensions are metaphysically distinct.

Nothing can be acquired without a person's *deed*, that is, her actual exercise of choice; but what is acquired can and must be conceived as acquired *for the first time*, which is "originally," at some point. Although this may sound like an interest in the history of acquisition of external things (as a chain of acquisition and transfer in time), Kant's preoccupation about first acquisition is a metaphysical-juridical problem. Kant has three analytical concerns in regard to the possibility of acquisition: firstly, to explain how an object can be acquired for the first time (original or first acquisition);[18] secondly, to account for the question of the *bindingness* of acquisition, since possession follows from an unilateral, contingent act (provisional acquisition); and thirdly, to explain how one's acquisition can be rightfully transferred from one person to another, that is, how one can acquire *derivatively* from the will of another (acquisition through transfer or derived acquisition from what belongs to another). While the latter (derived acquisition) requires in principle only the consenting will of the parties and is relatively unproblematic, first or original acquisition is theoretically more challenging. The problem is: How can acquisition that is not derived from the will of another be acquired ex nihilo from a legal perspective, and yet have legal consequences for the rights and duties of all other persons? Remember that all rights relations are relations between persons; if so, how can first acquisition be conceptualized as rightful? As we will see, Kant's solution to this problem is the view that acquisition in general must be regarded as approved ex ante by a community of all possessors ("those who possess in common"). The rational idea of a *community of the earth* allows unilateral appropriation to function as a valid principle of distribution in the state of nature, compatible with rightful relations between persons. The conclusive status of acquisition, however, will require an *instituted* community in the form of a civil condition, that is, a shared *positive* legal order. In the following, I will reconstruct each of these three analytic concerns in more detail.

---

[18] As we will see, first acquisition must be conceived as individual and unilateral; while other property arrangements are possible, Kant's point is that they must be conceived as "derived" from the first acquisition of individuals. Note that this is not a historical or genealogical account of acquisition, but a normative one. Possession can be held collectively if a group of possessors can be conceived as having consented to this property arrangement, or if their wills are "unified" under a common system of public laws. This is why national territory can be understood as the collective "possession" of its people, but only from an external – that is, international – perspective, since this is a right the people in question hold against outsiders, as is all the more relevant as long as a state of nature persists between national territories. See Pinheiro Walla (2020b).

3.1 Original or First Acquisition

> *A right to a thing* is a right to the private use of a thing of which I am in (original or instituted) possession in common with all others. For this possession in common is the only condition under which it is possible for me to exclude every other possessor from the private use of a thing (*ius contra quemlibet huius rei possessorem*)[19] since, unless such a possession in common is assumed, it is inconceivable how I, who am not in possession of the thing, could still be wronged by others who are in possession of it and are using it. – By my unilateral choice I cannot bind another to refrain from using a thing, an obligation he would not otherwise have; hence I can do this only through the united choice of all who possess it in common. Otherwise I would have to think of a right to a thing as if the thing had an obligation to me, from which my right against every other possessor of it is then derived; and this is an absurd way of representing it. (MS 6: 261)

Unless a person *already stands* in a juridically relevant relation with all other persons before she acquires something external for the first time, it is not possible to have a right against them in regard to one's acquisition. Consequently, that person cannot establish a *wrong (Läsion)* if someone else is empirically holding what she had first acquired. Common possession thus establishes a legal community as a rational idea. However, its role is not to account for the permission to divide the earth from a community of "proto-ownership" (Huber 2022, pp. 43–9). Common possession is what constitutes the *relational* character of original acquisition in Kant's legal theory; without the idea of an original community, one would have to understand possession primarily as a relation between a person and an object which can be "disturbed" by another's interference. In contrast, it is the rational idea of "the united choice of all those who possess in common," not one's particular relation to the object of acquisition, that establishes one's right to acquire for the first time. First acquisition particularizes that united choice of the original community, not primarily because there is a "permission to divide" the earth's resources, but because one already belongs to a legal community with all others in the first place.

Kant argues that the first acquisition of a thing can only be acquisition of land (MS 6: 261). The possibility of such acquisition is based on the original community of land in general:

> All human beings are originally (i.e., prior to any act of choice that establishes a right) in a possession of land that is in conformity with right, that is, they have a right to be wherever nature or chance (apart from their will) has placed

---

[19] A "right against whoever is the (empirical) possessor of this thing." Translated from Latin by Mary Gregor.

them. This kind of possession (*possessio*) – which is to be distinguished from residence (*sedes*), a chosen and therefore an acquired *lasting* possession – is a possession *in common* [*ein gemeinsamer Besitz*] because the spherical surface of the earth unites all the places on its surface [...]. (MS 6: 262)

Common possession of land gives rise to an *original* juridical community. "Original" means non-instituted, that is, not derived from someone's deed. Because this community is not constituted by a voluntary choice of its members, it must be conceptualized as logically prior to the acquisition of a determinate place on the earth. Note that this community is not imagined as a primordial moment in human history, but as a *rational idea*. The original community of land is *constructed* a priori, that is, formally, through the *logical relation* between all locations persons could occupy on the surface of the planet. Kant understands this logical relation between all possible locations on the planet as "disjunctively universal" (*disjunctiv-allgemein*).[20] It is "disjunctive" because if a person takes up a specific location on the earth, this very spot cannot be occupied by others at the same time; occupied locations are thus *mutually exclusive*. Nevertheless, all locations on the globe simultaneously coexist and are *interconnected*: no matter how far away from each other we may scatter, there is always the possibility of coming into contact or impacting each other in some way, whether intentionally or not. Consider, for instance the effects of climate change, which is a *global* problem: actions in one geographical area can causally affect all other parts of the planet (Pinheiro Walla, 2020a). The possibility of interaction is inevitable given the spherical, *bounded* surface of the Earth. The original community is therefore not a choice of those who come to occupy space on earth, but an involuntary form of interdependence structured by the planet's shape and its finitude. As Kant notes, the surface of the Earth as a whole has fixed dimensions, and is not capable of enlargement.[21] It is thus possible to conceive an involuntary "community of interaction," from the way all persons are confined with each other within a bounded planet. Although our locations are mutually exclusive, we are nevertheless *joined* together as an involuntary community of all potential occupants of the planet. Note that if this community is a rational idea, it means neither *us*, as the generation currently inhabiting the planet, nor an earlier generation at an imagined beginning of human history; instead, the community of the earth is a construct based on the idea of bounded (finite) space and the mutual exclusivity of points in that

---

[20] As noted by Byrd and Hruschka (2006, p. 263), translating "*disjunctiv-allgemein*" as "disjunctively universal" instead of "disjunctively general" is supported by Reflection 7942 (R 19: 561).

[21] "Alle Menschen auf Erden sind in einer ursprünglichen Gemeinschaft des Besitzes (communio originaria) des Erdbodens als eines Ganzen, welches seinem Umfange nach bestimmt und keiner Vergrößerung fähig ist." (Vor-PR 23: 322)

bounded space, both of which are essentially *contingent*. The locations one could come to occupy in that bounded space are in principle arbitrary.

The upshot is that my acquisition of a specific portion of land must be conceived as the appropriation of a *part of a determinate whole*. My possession (the "part") is thus something to which *every person had originally a right*, given the original community of land of the entire planet ("the determinate whole"). The fact that I appropriate a particular piece of land is thus *contingent*, given that anyone else would have the same legal capacity. This may sound puzzling to contemporary readers. Kant is not suggesting that everybody has an equal claim to what I possess, and therefore that my possession can be contested by everybody else. The argument is instead the following: I can only rightfully acquire for myself what everybody already had a right to originally, that is, *before* any acts of choice. This is required if I am to have a right I can hold against all other possessors, once I acquire something. If so, the main function of the original community of the earth in Kant's theory is to ensure that the *preliminary* normative conditions for a right *in rem* are in place. "Preliminary" because entering a condition of public law is also necessary and the next step for the possibility of a right *in rem*.

Another question remains: why do we need the idea of a "right to be somewhere," if the idea of a collective *Gesamtbesitz* seems sufficient to account for an original juridical community in regard to land? In other words, why does being "originally in possession of land with all other persons" amounts to "having a right to be wherever nature or chance (apart from one's will) has placed one"?

My answer is that representing the community of the earth as "disjunctively collective" allows Kant to reject the myth of a primordial communism of land found in his predecessors and embrace its normative function as a mere *schematization*. To elucidate my claim, let us consider two scenarios which would preclude the possibility of holding a right against all other persons, that is, a right *in rem*:

(1) if I do not stand in a juridical relation with them at all;
(2) if I stand in a juridical community with them, but this community is conceived as entailing *one single collective* right to all things, that is, it includes all persons on the globe as *a single right holder*.

If I am not *already* in common possession with all others before my unilateral acquisition, my actions can have no juridical significance in regard to them. This is because what establishes a right is one's legal standing in relation to other right holders, not one's actions as such. For my actions to become juridically relevant *deeds*, I must *already be in a* juridical relation with other persons, that is, in an original common possession with all others. Note that common possession for Kant is not a communism of external things. No external things have yet been *acquired*. The idea is merely that every person has a right to acquire as a *legal capacity*, not a claim-right to some acquisition. While this capacity is established *relationally*, this relation is constructed as spatial interconnection, that is, as the totality of potential locations on the planet. It is not surprising that original acquisition must be conceived as the acquisition of *land*, as a determinate area on the earth.

On the other hand, if I am already in a community of possession with all others, but the right to external things is conceived as being held together with all others as a collective, it would be impossible to conceive a wrong (*Läsion*) by one person against another. The concept of a right would become superfluous. As Byrd and Hruschka (2006) observe, "common possession does not mean that together [the members of the earth's community] have one right to possess the earth's surface as a community or society, because if the community includes everyone, then there is no one left against whom this right can be had" (p. 264); instead, common possession means merely the totality of each individual's *right to be somewhere*, understood as a capacity that is yet to be particularized by each individual person.[22] Therefore, first acquisition can only be individual (unilateral) and a part of what we all *already* possess in common and yet *disjunctively* (Kant's minimal and purely formal sense of possession in common). This is also why I am not wronging anyone when I appropriate a specific parcel of land for the first time, but can be wronged when another person interferes with my acquisition without my consent.

> All human beings are originally in *common possession* of the land of the entire earth (*communio fundi originaria*) and each has by nature the *will* to use it (*lex iusti*) which, because the choice of one is unavoidably opposed by nature to that of another, would do away with any use of it if this will did not also contain the principle for choice by which a *particular possession* for each on the common land could be determined (*lex iuridica*). But the law which is to determine for each what land is mine or yours will be in accordance with the axiom of outer freedom only if it proceeds from a will that is united *originally* and a priori (that presupposes no rightful act for its union). Hence it proceeds only from a will in the civil condition (*lex iustitiae distributivae*), which alone determines what is *right*, what is *rightful*, and what is *laid down as right*. – But in the former condition, that is, before the establishment of the civil condition but with a view to it, that is, *provisionally*, it is a *duty* to

---

[22] The same "right to be somewhere" applies to territorial states in regard to each other, since states are considered (to a certain extent) as analogous to *moral persons*. However, states presuppose individual choice and acquisition for their own constitution as civil conditions and for the delineation of their national territory.

proceed in accordance with the principle of external acquisition. Accordingly, there is also a rightful *capacity* of the will to bind everyone to recognize the act of taking possession and of appropriation as valid, even though it is only unilateral. Therefore provisional acquisition of land, together with all its rightful consequences, is possible. (MS 6: 267)

While the community of the earth allows us to justify possession "provisionally," "conclusive possession" is only possible under a civil constitution (MS 6: 264). What is the difference between provisional and conclusive possession? As I have argued elsewhere, the attributes "conclusive" or "peremptory" and "provisional" refer to the *modality* of one's title (Pinheiro Walla 2022). "Provisional" are rights whose status is still indeterminate from a public perspective, and thus open to contestation. In contrast, peremptory rights have a *conclusive* status. Competing rights claims are ruled out, because under a civil condition disputes are adjudicated by a public entity with the authority to decide, that is, with the legal power to bind all parties conclusively. Note that this is not primarily a matter of having the necessary coercive powers to enforce the right, but of normative authority to decide in a binding manner. Provisional rights are therefore rights in anticipation and expectation of a future civil condition (MS 6: 257), under which alone they can become conclusive, that is, *morally necessary*.[23]

3.2 Rights *In Rem* and Legal Closure

Despite its fundamental role for Kant's theory of acquisition, common possession of the earth does not satisfy the complete formal conditions for a right *in rem*. To this end, Kant introduces the argument for the duty to establish a civil condition, as the next argumentative step. But why is possession in common and the rational concept of a community of the earth not sufficient to account for the authority of the first and all subsequent possessors to impose an obligation on each other? Why is entering a civil condition with each other also required?

> The *empirical title* of acquisition was physical apprehension (*apprehensio physica*), based on the original community of land. Since there is only possession in *appearance* to put under possession in accordance with rational concepts of right, a title to take intellectual apprehension[24] (setting aside all empirical conditions of space and time) must correspond to this empirical title

---

[23] It is important not to confuse provisional rights with the idea of "temporary" or even "conditional" rights. For a criticism of interpretations of "provisionality" in Kant literature, see Pinheiro Walla (forthcoming).

[24] Kant uses here the expression *intellectuellen Besitznehmung* (literally: intellectual "taking of possession" or apprehension, as opposed to *intelligibler Besitz* (*possessio noumenon*). I have thus adapted Mary Gregor's translation by using "apprehension" as a translation of "Besitznehmung," in contrast to possession as a translation of "Besitz" This reflects the fact

of acquisition. This intellectual title is the basis of the proposition: 'What I bring under my control in accordance with laws of outer freedom and will to become mine becomes mine.' (MS 6: 264)

Physical apprehension is the subjective or *empirical* condition of possession. In order to be able to *use* an object, one must have the object under one's control. However, as previously stressed, holding the object does not yet constitute a *right* to that object. Physical apprehension of a thing must also be accompanied by an *intellectual* title. It is that intellectual title that allows us to think of the appropriated thing as a matter of *right*, which is, as a claim to the object that is independent of whether the possessor is presently empirically connected with the object. Intellectual apprehension is thus the *rational title* of acquisition, while physical apprehension is the empirical condition for the use of a thing. Therefore, more than empirical acquisition is necessary to ensure the normative conditions for the intellectual title. Kant now introduces the concept of an "a priori united will" which at first does not seem to be different from the rational concept of community of the earth:

> But the *rational title* of acquisition can lie only in the idea of a will of all united a priori (necessarily to be united), which is here tacitly assumed as a necessary condition (*conditio sine qua non*); for a unilateral will cannot put others under an obligation they would not otherwise have. – **But the condition in which the will of all is actually united for giving law is the civil condition.** Therefore something external can be *originally* acquired only in conformity with the idea of a civil condition, that is, **with a view to it and to its being brought about, but prior to its realization (for otherwise acquisition would be derived).** Hence *original* acquisition can only be *provisional*. – *Conclusive* acquisition takes place only in the civil condition. (MS 6: 264, my emphasis)

Although common possession of the earth provides a rightful basis for provisional acquisition in the state of nature, the institution of a civil condition is required for a *conclusive* title. Kant's argument for recognizing acquisition *prior* to the institution of the civil condition is motivated by an analytical concern: if acquisition was only possible once a civil condition has been instituted, all acquisition would be *derived*. We would not be able to account for original or first acquisition, that is, acquisition not derived from what *already* belongs to another. And yet there must be a first, underived acquisition, since persons do not have an innate right to anything external to themselves. This follows from the relational character of a Kantian conception of rights: objects outside persons are not constitutive of our external relations in

---

that mere rightful possession is now being applied to the context of acquisition (*Erwerbung*) and also matches the meaning suggested by the Latin terms used by Kant in parentheses.

a straightforward manner; they must be *acquired*, and their acquisition must somehow be able to generate rights and corresponding duties. A further argument for their incorporation into the sphere of rights is therefore needed.

While Kant's argument for provisional acquisition is based on *Vernunftrecht* ("right of reason," the "Kantianized" version of natural law theory), his argument for the civil condition and the need for positive laws shows that natural law theory is *insufficient* as a theory of legal obligation. In case of a dispute about rights in the state of nature, each person is at liberty (i.e., has *no duty not*) to follow their own best judgment on the matter. This liberty to decide in one's own case is characteristic of the state of nature; no one is *bound* to defer to another's judgment in matters of right, since in terms of authority to decide we all have the same status in regard to each other: we are *equals*. We now come to the question of *who has the authority* to settle the matter when two persons, who have an equal juridical status and liberty to think for themselves, disagree about rights (*quis iudicabit*?). Kant's answer is that for a conclusive verdict, both parties must thus stand under a common system of public laws with the authority to adjudicate on behalf of both parties in a way that is *equally binding* to each party. This ensures that no party is unilaterally imposing their own judgment about rights on the other, and thus acting in an asymmetric manner, violating the formal reciprocity requirement constitutive of juridical equality. The incompleteness of provisional acquisition thus reflects the limitations of natural law theory itself. Acquisition is provisional because without public authority and positive laws, it is not possible to preserve juridical equality in the face of disagreement about rights. This shortcoming gives rise to the *duty* to leave the state of nature. It also has significant implications for the possession of land and the territorial rights of states.

> Merely physical possession of land (holding it) **is already a right to a thing**, though certainly **not of itself sufficient for regarding it as mine**. Relative to others, since (as far as one knows) it is first possession, it is consistent with the principle of outer freedom and is also involved in original possession in common, which provides a priori the basis on which any private possession is possible. Accordingly, to interfere with the use of a piece of land by the first occupant of it **is to wrong him**. Taking first possession has therefore **a rightful basis** (*titulus possessionis*), which is original possession in common; and the saying "Happy are those who are in possession" (*beati possidentes*), because none is bound to certify his possession, is a basic principle of natural right, which lays down taking first possession as a rightful basis for acquisition on which every first possessor can rely. (MS 6: 251, my emphasis)

The very first act of acquisition must be conceived as acquisition of land. Until a civil condition is instituted, all possession of land is provisional, that is, its title is *inconclusive*, albeit *valid*. One could conclude that once a legal order has been established over a specific geographical area, the problem of provisional acquisition has been solved; acquisition now becomes conclusive. However, as long as the state of nature persists between legal orders, territorial rights continue to have provisional status from an international perspective. The title to territory remains empirical in regard to outsiders, and therefore normatively inconclusive (Ypi 2014). An immediate objection to this claim would be that territorial rights should not be treated in the same way as individual possession of land. The existence of an internal civil condition within a certain area should suffice for establishing territorial rights in regard to other groups. Kant suggests this when he rules out certain forms of international conduct towards states which were accepted in his lifetime, with the argument that they disrespect the internal union of its members and violate states' moral personality.[25] If so, there seems to be no need to expand the civil condition internationally for the sake of the territorial rights of existing states; the analogy with the argument for conclusive possession does not hold for territorial rights (Flikschuh 2010b, p. 480). The internal social contract and the moral personality of states, so the objection goes, replaces the idea that the title to national territory has provisional status requiring international law as a higher-level system of legal closure.

The internal civil condition and the moral personality of states do not exempt them from the duty to leave the state of nature. However, it introduces significant constraints on the way the duty to leave the international state of nature can be discharged. In contrast to individuals, who can be externally coerced to enter a civil condition (MS 6: 264), states must be able to *consent* to be bound by higher-order international and cosmopolitan legal orders (MS 6: 344, 351; ZeF 8: 357). One way to do this is by voluntarily becoming signatories of international treaties and conventions. There are two mutually related reasons for the consent condition for the *exeundum* at the international level. Firstly, if a group of states were to unilaterally force other states to join a single "world state", this could easily result in "the most fearful despotism" and be used as a tool for domination (TP 8: 311). Further, Kant thinks that by becoming too large,

---

[25] See the Second Preliminary Article for Perpetual Peace among states: "No independently existing state (whether small or large) shall be acquired by another state through inheritance, exchange, purchase or donation" (ZeF 8: 344). States are deemed "moral persons" in their external relations to other states, that is, in the international domain. According to Byrd (2006), Kant uses the term to indicate that, similarly to an individual, a state has perfect and imperfect duties towards itself (e.g., the perfect duty to preserve the civil condition against revolution and dissolution and the imperfect duty to reform its constitution to approach the republican ideal). It also has duties and rights against other states and its citizens. The moral personality of a state is constituted through the internal union of its members via the social contract.

a "universal monarchy" would weaken itself, and finally deteriorate into anarchy (ZeF 8: 367). Secondly, states already have a rightful constitution internally and consequently also have internal duties towards their own citizens by virtue of that internal social contract (ZeF 8: 355). These internal duties forbid states from instrumentalizing their own citizens, and constrain their external decisions, especially when it comes to employing their people to fight wars (TP 8: 311; ZeF 8: 344, 345, 350; MS §55 at 6: 344–6). While the duty to leave the international state of nature is not optional (an "optional duty" is an oxymoron in Kant's theory of obligation), it should not be externally imposed on states given their primary obligations to their own citizens and to protect their internal social contract. The condition thus introduces a *latitude* that is, a degree of flexibility in discharging the duty to leave the international state of nature, although no authorization to give up the required end altogether. On the other hand, Kant also believes, perhaps too optimistically, that, in the long run, the mechanism of nature or providence will lead states even *against* their will to enter a cosmopolitan constitution (TP 8: 310; ZeF 8: 361).[26]

> For they [the citizens of a state] must always be regarded as colegislating members of a state (not merely as means, but also as ends in themselves), and must therefore give their free assent, through their representatives, not only to waging war in general but also to each particular declaration of war. Only under this limiting condition can a state direct them to serve in a way full of danger to them.
>
> **We shall therefore have to derive this right** [to use citizens to fight a war] **from the *duty* of the sovereign to the people (not the reverse)**; and for this to be the case the people will have to be regarded as having given its vote to go to war. In this capacity it is, although passive (letting itself be disposed of), also active and represents the sovereign itself. (MS 6: 345–6, my emphasis)

If going to war can be compatible with or even directly required by what states owe to their own citizens as a matter of duty, the citizens of a state can be regarded as if they could have consented to go to war, and can be legitimately employed to defend their state. Note that Kant subverts Hobbes' idea that the sovereign has rights against the subjects, and that from this right the sovereign can employ them in war as he sees fit.[27] In Kant's account, it is the *duty* of the

---

[26] For an analysis of Kant's teleological views and perpetual peace, see Ypi (2010).

[27] Kant says "(...) I hope I will also be spared the reproach of overstating the case in favor of the people when I say that the people too has its inalienable rights against the head of state, although these cannot be coercive rights" (TP 8: 303–4). Hobbes is of the opposite opinion. According to him (1964, chapter 7, §14), "a head of state has no obligation to the people by the contract and cannot do a citizen any wrong (he may make what arrangements he wants about him). This proposition would be quite correct if a wrong were taken to mean an injury that gives the injured party a coercive right against the one who wronged him; but stated so generally, the proposition is appalling."

state towards its citizens that allows the state to draft its citizens to fight in a war of self-defense and impose danger on them, for the protection of their civil union. This condition also allows us to distinguish between the instrumentalization of the subjects for private purposes, and the legitimate employment of citizens as soldiers as compatible with their status as co-legislators in the civil union. Additionally, the consent condition of states to international law reflects the requirement that an international legal order that deserves the name must be compatible with the duties of states towards their own citizens. International law should not jeopardize these internal duties and expect states to sacrifice their own people or make them vulnerable to the violence and subjugation of others. Therefore, the internal duty of states to their citizens not only imposes constraints on states' decision-making at the international level, but also provides a *normative standard* for evaluating what can be externally expected from states internationally: the rights of states which arise from their internal civil condition. The consent condition also provides a guideline for ensuring the continuity and congruence between domestic and international legal orders, once these are implemented and expanded. Only then can states regard international law as *self-imposed* and (what may sound paradoxical to non-Kantians) as a *support* instead of a threat to self-determination.

4 International Law and *Rechtsstaatlichkeit*

> The right of *states* in relation to one another (which in German is called, not quite correctly, the *right of nations*, but should instead be called the right of states, *ius publicum civitatum*) is what we have to consider under the title the right of nations. Here a state, as a moral person, is considered as living in relation to another state in the condition of natural freedom and therefore in a condition of constant war. The rights of states consist, therefore, partly of their right *to go to* war, partly of their right *in* war, and **partly of their right to constrain each other to leave this condition of war and so form a constitution that will establish lasting peace** [*mithin eine den beharrlichen Frieden gründende Verfassung*), **that is, its right *after* war**. (6: 343, my emphasis)

A Kantian conception of international law, the *law of nations*, must start with the a priori legal principles that should regulate the external relations between states in the international state of nature. *Vernunftrecht* ("right of reason"), the nonpositive foundation of international law, takes into account as its point of departure and *modus operandi* the fact that there are no higher-order legal institutions regulating the interactions between sovereign states. Kant's aim is to spell out the minimally necessary institutional features of the international legal order according to *Vernunftrecht*, including the fundamental rational principles which should constitute the basis of any positive legal order. As Kant notes, although it is traditionally called "right of nations" (*Völkerrecht*), it should be properly understood as "the right of states" (*Staatenrecht*). The duty- and right-bearers in international law are states understood primarily as *legal orders*, not nations or peoples understood as ethnic or cultural groups (MS 6: 343).[28] States are treated, to a certain extent, in analogy to individuals in the state of nature: as mentioned before, states are considered "moral persons" having a claim to territorial integrity and self-determination, as well as duties towards their own subjects. Similarly to individuals in the state of nature, states also find themselves in a condition in regard to each other that is devoid of external laws. While the state of nature is considered a state of *war*, Kant differs from Hobbes in that he regards the very lawlessness of the state of nature as *wrong in itself*, regardless of the imminence or actual breakout of hostilities (MS 6: 344, 307–8). States thus have a duty to leave the state of nature with each other not just for prudential reasons, but because they already "do wrong *in the highest degree*" (*thun sie im höchsten Grade daran unrecht*) by merely wanting to *remain* in such a lawless condition (MS 6: 307).[29]

Kant's discussion of the law of nations comprises the rights states have in the international state of nature, restrictions on the permissible means to enforcing these rights, and finally the duty to leave the lawless condition at the international level. Importantly, the law of nations is not an instrument for justifying wars of aggression or state expansion, that is, a means for the acquisition of territory. Military force must be restricted to wars of self-defense in response to external aggression.[30] However, self-defense does not exhaust the law of nations. States also have other rights due to the legal *vacuum* of the state of nature. In case of rights disputes, states can mutually agree to go to war against each other to settle the matter. A war is technically a means of conflict resolution in the state of nature, where no binding adjudication organ is available, and states are at liberty to act as their own judges in rights disputes. However, Kant stresses that war is a barbaric means of conflict resolution (MS 6: 351; Ripstein 2021, p. 199). The question is how far waging war as conflict resolution would be compatible with states' duties towards their citizens, since self-defense may not be a clear objective of the rights dispute. In contrast, a distinctive feature of *peace* is that conflicts are settled

---

[28] For discussion, see Höffe (2006, p. 190) and Ripstein (2021).

[29] For an account of why it is wrong "in the highest degree" to stay in the state of nature, and Kant's distinction between formal wrongs (or "wrongs in general") and material wrongs, see Pinheiro Walla (2014) and Weinrib (2008).

[30] For a detailed analysis of national defense and the international legal order, see Ripstein (2021).

through legal procedure. Therefore, peace is only possible once the international state of nature has been overcome.

The right in war (*ius in bello*) is the most difficult aspect of the right of nations. While states are permitted to use any means required for self-defense that "does not render their subjects unfit to be citizens," they must not use "underhanded means as would destroy the trust requisite to establishing a lasting peace in the future" (MS 6: 347). Conduct in war must be such as not to undermine the possibility of leaving the state of nature with each other. This condition imposes significant constraints on the methods of war; while states are *not forbidden* to settle rights disputes through war, given the absence of an international legal order with the authority to issue a binding verdict on such disputes, war must always be waged with a view to the possibility of a future and lasting peace. Stratagems that perpetuate the state of nature by undermining trust and rendering reconciliation impossible are thus impermissible.

While ensuring that peace remains at least possible in the future is a *negative* measure, the *positive* step towards peace lies in the implementation of an international legal order, which ideally would approximate as much as possible the structure of domestic legal orders while averting the danger of global-scale despotism. The preliminary configuration for an international legal order is thus a *federalism* of *republican states*, whose function is to provide mutual security from the external attacks of states and groups which are not members of the federation of states. The members of the federation of states are committed both to refraining from mutual aggression, as well as to mutual military assistance in case of external threats to one of its members. States qualified to become members of the federation of states must be *republics* internally. Therefore, the first positive step towards an international legal order requires states that are *well-ordered internally*. It is essential that the member states possess what Kant calls a republican constitution.

In a broader sense, a republic is the form of an association "by which all are united through their common interest in being in a rightful condition" (MS 6: 311). Because of its form, a republican state is thus called a "commonwealth (*res publica latius sic dicta*)" (MS 6: 311). In a strict sense, however, a republic is a *representative* form of government (MS 6: 341). It separates the executive from the legislative power. Its constitution is also the only one that accords with right; unlike other constitutions that serve merely to bring about the submission of the subjects, the form of the republican constitution, which reflects the idea of the original contract, makes the principle of external freedom the condition for the exercise of coercion. (MS 6: 340). Therefore, the possibility of exiting the federation of states also reflects the fact that states are "works in progress" when it comes to approaching the ideal republican constitution. International law itself is ongoing and developing. International law thus requires a certain degree of juridical progress domestically, although principles of international law can also play an important role in incentivizing and guiding domestic reforms as a condition for membership.

Further, the federation Kant envisions is not supposed to be a federal state; it is rather a *confederation*, which presupposes the continued existence of sovereign states, not their dissolution into a world state (Lauterpacht 1977 / 1945, pp. 19, 25). However, proper state building should naturally lead a state to join the law of nations (Capps and Rivers 2010). International law and *Rechtsstaatlichkeit* – or "the rule of law" – are thus interconnected. Their relationship can be understood as the result of a consistency requirement; international law is necessary from the perspective of internal legal orders because remaining in the international state of nature is a wrong *in itself*, and to the highest degree. If so, the problem cannot be solved at the domestic level alone. It calls for an *international* rule of law.

> There are no limits to the rights of a state against an *unjust enemy* **(no limits with respect to quantity or degree, though there are limits with respect to quality)**; that is to say, an injured state may not use *any* means *whatever* but may use those means that are allowable to any degree that it is able to, in order to maintain what belongs to it. – But what is an *unjust enemy* in terms of the concepts of the right of nations, in which – as is the case in a state of nature generally – each state is judge in its own case? It is an enemy whose publicly expressed will (whether by word or deed) reveals a maxim by which, if it were made a universal rule, any condition of peace among nations would be impossible and, instead, a state of nature would be perpetuated. (MS 6: 369, my emphasis)

It seems impossible to identify an unjust aggressor in the international state of nature. Since it is by definition a state of anarchy, under which each state is justified to follow its own judgments about rights, it seems that no one can be declared "unjust" unless by another, equally unilateral judgment.[31] A particular state has no more power to bind another state by its unilateral judgment than the other state would have to bind them in return. Kant however provides a standard for defining an unjust aggressor in the state of nature, analogously to his distinction between wrongs in general (*Unrecht überhaupt*), and particular wrongs (MS 6: 307–8).[32] An unjust enemy is one who acts in such a way as

---

[31] This is because even though states are themselves public legal orders internally, they are equals in regard to each other.

[32] "Men do one another no wrong at all when they feud among themselves; for what holds for one holds also in turn for the other, as if by mutual consent ... But in general they do wrong in the

to undermine the possibility of a future peace, and thus perpetuates the logic of the state of nature. Therefore, resisting that enemy is justified not only because doing so is not inconsistent with the juridical vacuum of the state of nature, but as a prerogative of right. A prerogative of right is a normative standard that allows us to identify conduct that is favored by reason because it is not only compatible with but also prepares the ground for an international legal order. Possession in the state of nature has in its favor the rightful presumption that it will be made into rightful possession through public lawgiving. It therefore holds "comparatively as rightful possession" in anticipation of a rightful condition (MS 6: 257). A similar presumption applies to conduct in the international domain that is compatible with and anticipates a civil condition between states. *Exeundum esse e statu naturali*; those whose conduct paves the way towards overcoming the international state of nature have right on their side.

> Since a state of nature among nations, like a state of nature among individual human beings, is a condition that one ought to leave in order to enter a lawful condition, before this happens any rights of nations, and anything external that is mine or yours which states can acquire or retain by war, are merely *provisional*. Only in a universal *association of states* (analogous to that by which a people becomes a state) can rights come to hold *conclusively* and a true *condition of peace* come about. (MS 6: 350)

5 What Is an International Civil Condition?

What does it mean to "leave the state of nature" at the international level? And what would an international legal order entail from a Kantian perspective? Kant did not offer much detail about how an international legal order would relate to domestic legal orders, and even less about its implications for domestic property rights systems. In this section, I will use Hans Kelsen's idea of the *cognitive unity of law* to elaborate on how the relation between international and domestic legal orders could be understood from a Kantian perspective. My discussion of Kelsen's theory will therefore be restricted to those aspects I believe can help elucidate and complement Kant's conception of an international legal order.[33] I also reflect on how Kelsen's monism about international law would apply to property rights, and its repercussions for diverse domestic property systems as

---

highest degree by willing to be and to remain in a condition that is not rightful, that is, in which no one is assured of what is his against violence."

[33] Corradetti (2020) also brings together Kant and Kelsen on the unity of law and international law. However, Corradetti's emphasis is on Kelsen's views about "psychological" coercion, that is, the possibility of states' *voluntary* obedience to international law, given the lack of an international sanctioning system of compliance, which he develops into a Kantian reading that attempts to make sense of Kant's puzzling statements about the league of states (p. 189–190). I return to Corradetti's interpretation later in this section.

they may be encountered in different societies and cultures, and again draw a comparison to Kant's position.

As a starting point, it is helpful to recall the "circumstances" of international law, that is, the background conditions under which the problem of "right between states" arises. The international domain is characterized by a plurality of sovereign states in a lawless state in regard to each other, that is, they share no legal order with each other. However, one could object that this state of nature is not absolute. This was true even in Kant's time, since treaty law was already in existence, however limited and fragile. Kant laments the state of international treaties of his time when he criticizes "mental reservations" in the making of peace treaties, which so often turned peace agreements into mere temporary truces, as opposed to lasting peace (ZeF 8: 343–4). In light of this, we can safely assume that the international order of Kant's time was regulated to a limited extent by some publicly recognized norms. These norms of international law are rules for the regulation of interstate relations; they impose duties and recognize rights for states as legal persons in the international domain, and to individuals insofar as they act as state representatives or are members of their particular states. One of the fundamental principles of international law is *pacta sunt servanda,* according to which agreements are the source of binding obligations, and ought to be fulfilled in good faith (Lukashuk 1989).[34]

The norms of international law were created by the voluntary acts of particular states, established through their reciprocal behavior towards each other, and ultimately consolidated through *custom*. Their scope of validity is necessarily limited; treaty law does not apply to all states across the board, but only to those directly involved in a particular agreement. As Kelsen (1997) observed, characteristic of the initial stage of international law development is the decentralized creation and application of norms, in contrast to domestic norm creation by states as centralized legal orders. Consequently, the international legal community is *fragmented*, operating as isolated pockets in international law creation. Kelsen named this stage of development "international law as a primitive legal system" (p. 109).

Further development of international law would entail the gradual centralization of the creation and application of international law, starting with adjudication. While these functions would initially take place within specific legal communities, the aim would be to expand the scope of international jurisdiction towards a *global* legal community, similarly to the development of state legal

---

[34] See MS 6: 219. Kant uses *pacta sunt servanda* as an example of a duty based on juridical lawgiving (*Ius*). Although ethics also commands that I fulfil a contract I entered into, the duty is itself juridical in nature.

systems themselves, but at a more gradual pace, and with the cooperation of states themselves. Since Kelsen considers coercion the distinctive feature of law as opposed to other normative domains such as morality or religion, international law would also require external sanctions. If so, would an international legal order amount to a world state in Kelsen's conception, that is, a centralized legal order with coercive powers, similarly to an individual state?

At first sight, Kelsen's approach does not seem compatible with Kant's treatment of international law, especially if we bear in mind Kant's reservations about a world state. Kelsen also criticized Kant for allegedly failing to live up to the standards of his own critical philosophy, and allowing metaphysics into his practical philosophy (Kelsen 1997 / 1934, p. xxix). Therefore, it would be natural to assume that Kelsen offers a *refutation* of Kant's account of international law rather than an *extension* of Kant's views, as I am suggesting. However, it is important to bear in mind that the departing point for Kelsen's theory of international law is Kant's *critical philosophy*, not Kant's legal theory.[35] Kelsen's "pure theory of law" is guided by fundamental insights of Kant's transcendental idealism (von Daniels 2019). While Kelsen's account could be understood as a critique of Kant's conception of international law, this will depend on how one interprets Kant's legal philosophy.[36] My view is that Kant's position in regard to the relation between natural law and positive law is more sophisticated than Kelsen assumed: legal positivism is *required* by *Vernunftrecht*. The view I will defend here is that Kant offers a natural law argument for legal positivism. The idea is that a public system of laws that operates according to its own internal principles of validity is the solution to the problem identified in the state of nature. Positive laws ensure that all persons are equally subjected to the law and symmetrically situated in regard to each other. I will say more about Kant's own brand of legal positivism in Section 7. In the following, I will reconstruct Kelsen's epistemic argument for international law and use its insights to elaborate a Kantian conception of the international law system. This conception will also take into account Kant's concerns about the dangers of a world state and of becoming a mere instrument for enforcing the prejudices and political interests of particular states.

Kelsen (1997 / 1934) distinguishes between two concepts of unity: cognitive and organizational (pp. 123–4). As he observes, law must be conceived as a unified system: "legal cognition" strives to represent its object as an unity

---

[35] In this, Kelsen can be compared to John Rawls, who approached Kant's political philosophy not from the perspective of Kant's legal-political writings themselves, but on the basis of Kant's *moral* philosophy. On Rawls' "applied ethics" approach to Kant's political philosophy, see Ripstein (2009, chapter one).

[36] I would like to thank an anonymous referee for pressing me to clarify this point.

(1997 / 1934, p. 111). If we assume that international law and a plurality of state legal systems constitute not only independent but mutually exclusive systems of laws (based on two distinct "basic norms"), unification seems incompatible with the sovereignty of states. Kelsen criticizes the "dogma" of state sovereignty and argues that there is in fact no logical contradiction between international and state law:

> One cannot claim that a norm with content A is valid, and claim at the same time that a norm with content not-A is valid. One can claim – and no doubt must claim, in view of the facts – that norms whose content is mutually exclusive actually are issued and, on the part of the norm-addressees, are imagined and are obeyed or not obeyed. There is no more a logical contradiction in this statement, referring to natural facts, than there is in the observation that two opposing forces are both efficacious. But one cannot claim that two norms whose content is, logically speaking, mutually exclusive are valid at the same time – that is, one cannot claim that A ought to be and, at the same time, not-A ought to be, just as one cannot claim that A is and, at the same time, not-A is.
>
> If legal cognition encounters legal norms that contradict one another in content, it seeks, by interpreting their meaning, to resolve the contradiction as a mere pseudo-contradiction. If this effort fails, legal cognition disposes of the material to be interpreted, disposes of it as lacking in meaning altogether and therefore as non-existent in the legal sphere qua realm of meaning. What is established thereby is simply a predisposition inherent in legal cognition, [a predisposition in favour of unity]. (1997 / 1934, p. 111)[37]

At the heart of Kelsen's monism is the idea that cognitive unity is epistemically necessary for law; it functions as a regulative ideal for legal cognition, and provides a framework for overcoming tensions between incompatible norms. Although the content of two norms may contradict each other, there are ways, internal to legal systems themselves, to deal with such contradictions. For this, the international and the domestic system must be viewed as a unified, single legal order (Jakab 2004). Unlike what one could naturally assume, international law does not offer a standard of validity for state law; instead, international law presupposes the legitimacy of states as legal orders, in accordance with the so-called principle of effectiveness. A state is considered legitimate by international law simply by being able "to secure continuous obedience to the norms it issues" (Kelsen 1997 / 1934, p. 120).[38] Therefore,

---

[37] Similarly, many valid moves in baseball are incompatible with other valid moves in the game. This does not undercut the validity of the rules behind these moves. I would like to thank Stefan Sciaraffa for suggesting this comparison.

[38] This is also compatible with Kant's own position on the legitimacy of a state. The legitimacy of a state is not dependent on whether it is perfectly just, or historically just in its origins. See MS 6: 318, General Remark A.

tensions between international and national legal norms do not imply that a national norm or the legal system as a whole is invalidated by international law. Kelsen's criticism of the traditional concept of sovereignty ("the dogma of sovereignty") is thus epistemological. It arises from the insight that sovereignty as a normative legal concept cannot be derived from the fact that states *happen* to be independent and refuse to bind themselves by external norms in the international domain. Kelsen's criticism is the rejection of a naturalistic fallacy in legal theory.

However, and most importantly for his argument, Kelsen contends that the jurisdictional competence of a state does not reach beyond the sphere of validity of that state's legal system. This poses an unexpected authority problem for international treaty creation: A treaty imposes duties on and grants rights to the states involved in creating the treaty. Although these duties and rights will apply to the respective sphere of validity of each of the states involved (internally), the mere unilateral will of the parties lacks the competence to impose duties outside their own jurisdiction (externally). Therefore, a higher-order legal norm is *formally* required to establish the competence of the involved states to create norms via treaty-making.[39]

> The creation of norms of international law can be theoretically comprehended only from the standpoint of general international law, which governs such law creation by qualifying the state treaty in particular as a law-creating method, that is, by obligating the states to act in accordance with treaty. From this standpoint, the state representatives who are active in concluding a treaty between their two states make up a compound but unitary organ, an organ of the community of states constituted by general international law, and not, say, a common organ of both states. Power is delegated by international law to the state legal system to determine which individual is to express, in the name of the state, the state's will vis-à-vis the treaty; and therefore the state representatives active in concluding the treaty are, as suborgans of the collective organ creating the treaty norm, primarily organs of the international legal community. Each of these suborgans is only secondarily an organ of its own state. Thus, it is not really individual states that create international law by way of treaty, as those writers influenced by the dogma of sovereignty usually stress; rather, it is the community of states or, more correctly, the international legal community – just as it is the state that creates state law by way of state organs. (Kelsen 1997 / 1934, p. 123)

---

[39] Kelsen's position amounts to rejecting the view that international law is the "private law of states," according to which states are comparable to private persons in the international state of nature (for a discussion of the latter position, see Ripstein 2019). Kelsen's insight is that international law must be *public law* from the very start in order to be binding.

We tend to assume that "the united wills" of states can give rise to valid norms for both parties, similarly to contractual agreements between two individuals in the state of nature (which Kant would categorize as *Privatrecht*, "private right"). However, from a legal-positivist perspective, the aggregate wills of two states is not sufficient for this; a higher-order legal system is, in fact, necessary to create the norms according to which treaties can be created between states and have binding force. This higher-order system is constituted by the international legal community itself, and not by states in isolation.

Kelsen's legal monism bears resemblance to Kant's argument for international law as required by domestic property rights. Also, Kant's distinctive version of legal positivism has some affinities with Kelsen's legal positivism, despite Kelsen's contentions about Kant's metaphysical assumptions. As mentioned earlier, Kant's legal positivism is motivated by *Vernunftrecht*, which can be understood as Kant's version and correction of traditional natural law theory. Kant's paradoxical-sounding position is that legal positivism is the solution to a problem identified by *Vernunftrecht*, given the "circumstances of justice" in the state of nature; omnilaterality in external relations is only possible under a public law system that operates within its own sphere of validity, that is, *procedurally*, in accordance with its own internal public standards. Only in this way can all persons be equally situated under the law and in regard to each other, no one above the law. But the commitment to positive laws always comes with a certain price; one must follow procedure and the rule of law even when it departs from our private judgments about what is just in a certain situation. Dispensing with procedure whenever one disagrees with its substantive outcomes would amount to rendering the positive system of laws superfluous, and reintroduce the problems which necessitated the duty to leave the state of nature in the first place.

This legal-positivistic aspect of Kant's legal theory is particularly visible in his discussion of equity (*Billigkeit*, MS 6: 234–5) and instances where he insists on the validity of a decision of a court of justice even though it contradicts individuals' judgments about justice ("On acquisition that is dependent subjectively upon the decision of a court of justice," §§36–40, MS 6: 296–305). Individual judgments about rights are said to be "objective" when they follow a priori legal principles as they would apply in the state of nature. Despite being "objective," these judgments are nevertheless *private* from a legal perspective, and cannot bind others externally. Once in a civil condition, one must defer to the "subjective" verdict of a court of justice as binding. These verdicts are "subjective" because they are derived from the application of public laws and statutes, which are *empirical* principles, and follow established legal procedure. This means that given the procedural constraints a court is subject to, its verdicts may not coincide with individual judgments about rights. Kant thus distinguishes between two forms of legal reasoning: legal reasoning in the state of nature (in accordance with a priori legal principles) and legal reasoning by a court of justice (which is bound by the positive laws and procedure of a concrete, historically given legal system). Kant endorses the "separability thesis" between law and morality as essential for the functioning and preservation of positive systems of laws. He does not deny that the judgment of a court of justice can depart from individual judgment about rights and still be valid. Although positive laws are binding, the tension between the two forms of legal reasoning seems to be ineradicable.[40] Like legal positivists after him, Kant did not seek to eliminate the tension between positive laws and morality (cf. Hart 1958). It is plausible to assume that Kant also regarded the tensions between positive law and morality as productive, since they can be used to guide reforms and improve legal systems (cf. Williams 2001). I discuss Kant's legal positivism in more detail in Section 7.

Let us return to the question of the nature of an international legal order from a Kantian perspective. While it is natural to conflate the notion of a civil condition with the implementation of a state, a legal order does not require the replication of state structures. A formal argument can be made in support of this point: were international law to lead to the implementation of a world state, it would ultimately turn international law into *domestic law*; it would abolish international law altogether. Therefore, it is sufficient to achieve a *relatively* centralized international legal order. As Leben (1998) put it in regard to the European Union as a possible model for international law, it is "less than a state order but more [centralized] than that of any other international organization" (p. 298). While states must agree to subject themselves to rules, a supranational sovereign with moral personality is not required for satisfying the duty to leave the international state of nature. Further, this is compatible with the possibility of external coercion at the international level, provided states have previously consented to submit themselves to the jurisdiction of international law entities, which they bring about initially through international treaties. Kant's position has affinities with current constitutionalism debates, which stress that there can be no self-standing national constitutional legitimacy without embedment within a wider, international legal system (Kumm 2013; see also Koskenniemi 2007).

But how to reconcile the idea of "Kantian cosmopolitan constitutionalism" with the constraint that states must not be externally coerced to comply with

---

[40] For a discussion of equity and its relationship to public law in Kant's legal theory, see Pinheiro Walla (2019).

international law? A suggestion recently advanced in Kant scholarship is some form of *internalization* of the norms of international law into the constitution of states. Claudio Corradetti (2021) proposes a "transitional" interpretation of the federation of states and of the world republic (*Weltrepublik*) as a *regulative idea of reason*, according to which international law would function as a normative standard *guiding* the behavior of states domestically, while falling short of constituting an external system of law with coercive powers:

> States adopt laws, judicial decisions, etc. issued by a supra-ordinate political entity only 'as if' they were externally coerced to do so. In fact, however, they maintain an always actionable opting-out reservation in regard to the demands of an international body. Suppose that international obligations are regulated and enforceable. This means that states' compliance with the commands of an external agency would occur 'as if' there was an external enforcement. In fact, though, actual enforceability is left to states' exercises of sovereign will and to their understanding of the compulsory character of non-domestic law in regulative terms. (p. 186)

Corradetti (2017) puts forward a Kantian theory of *transitionality* as "a political approximation to peace" (p. 416). He explains how the increasing juridification of the international domain can be implemented in a way that is compatible with the constraints imposed by the moral personality of states. Instead of implementing a coercive international system of laws, which would presumably eliminate pluralism at the international level, Corradetti proposes a "symbolic constitutionalism," whose organizational paradigm is an "as if" reasoning on the part of states. States would therefore internalize international laws as guidelines to their own behavior to be enforced *through state law*. A similar view has also been put forward by Jakob Huber (2022):

> A cosmopolitically transformed state acknowledges obligations of international and cosmopolitan right: it binds itself to interact with other states or individuals on peaceful terms and binds its citizens to do so with distant strangers. In the absence of a coercive form of global government, transforming states into outward-looking, cosmopolitan agents is the most promising – in fact, the only viable – strategy for finding peaceful terms of engagement with other states and non-state peoples. (p. 147)

Kant stressed that the *real* states of his time held a very different conception of the law of nations from the ideal conception required by reason. However, the tension between "theory" and "practice" was not due to an alleged failure of philosophical theories to apply to real-life politics ("it may be correct in theory, but is no good in practice!"), but the *de facto* unwillingness of states to sacrifice political interests, that is, their unbounded liberty in the international domain.[41] Kant's diagnosis was that the states of his time rejected *in hypothesi* (in their actual behavior) what is correct *in thesi* (in theory) (ZeF 8: 357).[42] It is therefore helpful to distinguish between an *ideal* and a *realist* meaning of "sovereignty." While Kant has the ideal meaning in mind when he talks about states as "moral persons" who represent and have duties to their own people and should therefore be free from instrumentalization and domination from other states, he has the *realist* meaning in mind when he mentions the unwillingness of states to be restrained by international law because it would be an impediment to the advancement their political interests. Therefore, state sovereignty and international law contradict each other only from the perspective of *Realpolitik*, or the *realist* concept of sovereignty, which adopts a radically different fundamental political maxim from the ideal concept of sovereignty. Kant characterized each of these maxims as a matter of hierarchy between morality and politics, with the "moral politician" setting morality above politics, and the "political moralist" subordinating morality to politics (ZeF 8: 372).[43] However, the talk of "morality" imposing constraints on politics is misleading and requires qualification, since it suggests that *ethical* principles instead of *juridical* principles should regulate states' conduct in the international domain. Kant is not offering a doctrine of virtue for states, but arguing for the necessity and primacy of international law.[44] Further, it seems implausible to assume that the challenges concerning the implementation of international law should have led Kant to change its status from Right (*Recht*) to Virtue (*Tugend*), since both domains of Morals (understood broadly as *Sitten*) have different corresponding lawgiving principles (*Gesetzgebung*): the principle of Right dealing with external

---

[41] In order to avoid ambiguity when talking about states' interests, it is important to note that Kant distinguishes between the *private* interests of rulers that benefit from anarchy in the international domain and the *duties* of states towards their own citizens. The former provide rulers with incentives to perpetuate lawlessness in the international domain and undermine the prospects for peace. In contrast, the duties of states towards their citizens can also be called "interests" of states in the international domain, since they are just as uncoerced to act as they see fit in the international state of nature as their rogue counterparts. From a formal perspective, both "interests" have the same status, since states are equally at liberty to follow their own private judgments in the international state of nature (both are *sovereign* states). However, the state which lives up to its duties towards its own citizens has the prerogative of right on its side, and its conduct is compatible with Right.

[42] See also Corradetti (2021, p. 190) and my discussion of the *in thesi* / *in hypothesi* distinction and realist elements in Kant's legal thought in Pinheiro Walla (2017).

[43] Cf. Kelsen's account of the hierarchy relations between domestic and international law discussed below.

[44] International order should be developed gradually and *dynamically*. If developed organically from the inner constitution of states it will no longer be perceived as intrusive or as imposed "from above"; international law would be instead the expression of the united will of all states, and not an instrument for some states to pursue their political agendas against others.

freedom, while the principle of Virtue has to do with internal freedom (MS 6: 406–7).[45]

It is possible to draw an analogy between Kant's realist concept of sovereignty and Kelsen's critique of legal *dualism*. According to this analogy, Kant and Kelsen share the insight that political realism and legal dualism respectively are *inconsistent* positions,[46] indeed possible to adopt *in practice* but only by denying "what is correct in theory," that is, what is *rationally required* by the very concept of a public system of laws.[47]

In the *Pure Theory of Law,* Kelsen (1967 / 1960) discusses two possible monistic constructions, each one defined by a specific hierarchy relation between national and international legal orders. Either the national legal order has priority over international law, or international law is regarded as having primacy over domestic law (§43d). If one presupposes the validity of international law . . .

> . . . the question arises how from this starting point the validity of the national legal order can be established; in that case the reason for the validity of this order must be found in international law. This is possible, because, as we mentioned in a different context [§34 h], the principle of effectiveness (which is the norm of positive international law), determines both the reason for the validity and the territorial, personal and temporal sphere of validity of the national legal orders; and these, therefore, may be conceived as being delegated by international law and therefore subordinated to it – conceived, in other words, as partial legal orders included in a universal world legal order; the coexistence of the national legal orders in space and their succession in time is then made legally possible by international law.

The argument is that international law is normatively required for the validity of a national legal order because a national order itself cannot account for its own validity beyond its own jurisdictional scope, that is, in regard to other legal

---

[45] See also MS 6: 218–21 and MS 6: 231. There is an extensive debate in Kant scholarship about the relationship between Right and Virtue in Kant's theory. See, for instance, Willaschek (1997), Baiasu (2016), and Horn (2014). My view is that while Morality (*Sitten*) is a unified whole under the idea of freedom, Right (*Recht*) and Virtue or Ethics (*Tugend*) correspond to freedom in external and internal perspectives, respectively. Both domains are integrated within a unified system of freedom but ultimately autonomous within their respective spheres of application or "jurisdiction." Cf. Guyer (2002).

[46] For an argument that legal dualism is inconsistent, see Dyzenhaus (2018).

[47] See ZeF 8: 356: "It is understandable for a people to say, 'There shall be no war among us; for we want to form ourselves into a state, that is, to establish for ourselves a supreme legislative, executive, and judicial power, which settles our disputes peaceably.' But if this state says, 'There shall be no war between myself and other states, although I recognize no supreme legislative power which secures my right to me and to which I secure its right,' it is not understandable on what I want to base my confidence in my right, unless it is the surrogate of the civil social union, namely the free federalism that reason must connect necessarily with the concept of the right of nations if this is to retain any meaning at all."

orders, over which it has no authority. After all, particular states are all *partial* legal orders in regard to each other. The assumption that states are "moral persons", that is, that their internal constitution somehow qualifies them to function as independent sources of obligations internationally tends to obscure the role of international law in validating national legal orders.[48] The recognition of state validity by international law through the principle of effectiveness encompasses a state's territory and its specific property rights system, whatever the latter happens to be. International law does not prescribe content to private law domestically; it *recognizes it* within a universal world legal order.

As genuine law, international law is by definition a coercive system. In its decentralized stage of development, the sanctions of international law consist of reprisals and war (Kelsen 1967 / 1960, §42a, p. 322). However, the use of force in the international domain can only be understood either as a sanction or as a delict (p. 321); the latter is an action that constitutes a *condition* for the application of international sanctions. Therefore, even at its primitive level of development, international law asserts that there is no right to wage war indiscriminately; consequently, the international community is no longer in a state of complete lawlessness. Although Kelsen thus reaffirms here the *bellum iustum* tradition, his aim is not to justify the just war as the *definitive* conception of international law; rather, Kelsen suggests that there is a way to improve interstate relations, namely, through the expansion of international law. The difference between a primitive international legal order and an advanced legal order is a matter of *degree* (Leben 1998, p. 289). Kelsen's conception of international law is *dynamic*: it proposes the gradual centralization of law, starting with adjudication, in the form of international courts. These international institutions, however, cannot be a mere tool for states to feud against each other or instruments for the pursuit of political ideologies, since this would reaffirm the primacy of national law over international law. On the contrary, international law must genuinely constitute a higher-level legal order subordinating all states equally under the international rule of law. This is an ideal the international community must strive towards, and by no means corresponds to the reality of current international law and international institutions.

An objection raised against legal monism is that it is a faulty theory at both descriptive and normative levels. It is descriptively faulty because it cannot account for the diversity of property regimes in developing countries, and how informal property rules are developed by marginalized groups; it is normatively faulty because it denies normative relevance to this diversity of property regimes (Bonilla Maldonado 2009, p. 214).

---

[48] This holds true also of Kant's *Völkerrecht*.

Kelsen regards specific property systems as ideological in nature (Kelsen 1967 / 1960, §29b). In fact, Kelsen does not consider the implementation of subjective rights, that is, the legal power of individuals to make legal claims against others, as the essential function of the law. Instead, the fundamental role of the law is the establishment of *legal obligations* (p. 136). The emphasis is thus primarily on legal duties rather than rights, suggesting another commonality with Kant's legal theory. The Pure Theory of Law does not give preference to any specific system of rights over another, since preference can only be a political, that is, ideological choice, and beyond the scope of the theory, as Kelsen conceives it. Because the Pure Theory of Law must remain committed to value-neutrality as much as possible, it must also incorporate diverse legal systems and adopt a stance that I will call "pragmatic relativism" (since value relativism per se would presuppose a metaphysical commitment, and would itself not be itself value-neutral). The theory does not necessarily rule out political choices in the implementation of legal systems either, but stresses the importance of being *conscious* that we are dealing with a political choice, lest law be confused with other normative domains. It follows that the Pure Theory of Law's regulative commitment to value-neutrality does not require it to abolish ideologically diverse legal systems. As a scientific methodology, value-neutrality allows the Pure Theory of Law to identify ideology and be critical of it (Dedek 2021).

As we saw earlier, Kant's argument about provisional acquisition of property necessarily leads domestic legal orders towards international law. Kant's argument starts with a reference to the planet as constituting a global legal community, the "community of the earth," and culminates in the requirement to implement a global civil condition (which Kant seems to walk back from when it comes to its *implementation*, while acknowledging that this is what *reason* requires). The result of this impasse is a "second best option," falling short of a world state, but still a form of international institution, namely a federation of states. It is therefore not only possible but indeed *required* that states submit to international law in due time and in some form, and continuously work towards improving it and gradually approaching the Kantian ideal.

Kant's argument for the need to move from provisional to peremptory acquisition forces us to think about property rights and possession of land from an international perspective. The very possibility of a right *in rem* requires a civil condition with a global scope (Byrd & Hruschka 2006). Because the right to acquire external objects, including land, takes place within the framework of the original community of the earth, the *validity* of acquisition must have a *global character*. However, Kant is not committed to implementing any specific conception of property rights, despite often discussing individual rights as understood within the liberal tradition. For instance, Kant acknowledges the territorial claims of nomadic people and takes into account their specific way of making use of the territory as establishing collective possession:

> Again, can anyone have a thing as his own on land no part of which belongs to someone?
> Yes, as in Mongolia where, since all the land belongs to the people, the use of it belongs to each individual, so that anyone can leave his pack lying on it or recover possession of his horse if it runs away, since it is his. On the other hand, it is only by means of a contract that anyone can have a movable thing as his on land that belongs to another. (MS 6: 225–6)

And later:

> All land belongs only to the people (and indeed to the people taken distributively, not collectively), except in the case of a nomadic people under a sovereign, with whom there is no private ownership of land. (MS 6: 324)

Kant also recognizes diversity of ways of life and the way it can determine how peoples use their land. This is relevant for establishing a sign that the people is de facto in possession of a specific territory and their title against other contenders to the land. Kant's assumption is that evaluating ways of life is not the business of *Recht*; as a *choice* of the community, it must be respected by outsiders, provided everybody keeps within their own boundaries and does not interfere with another's territory and differing ways of life:

> Finally, can two neighboring peoples (or families) resist each other in adopting a certain use of land, for example, can a hunting people resist a pasturing people or a farming people, or the latter resist a people that wants to plant orchards, and so forth. Certainly, since as long as they keep within their boundaries the way they want to live on their land is up to their own discretion (*res merae facultatis*). (M 6: 225–6)

While a transitional approach to international law is important, "symbolic" and "as-if" interpretations of Kantian global constitutionalism are ultimately insufficient for the legal closure required for rights *in rem* and for territorial rights. Lasting peace, which is the ultimate aim of international law, can only be effectively achieved through a mechanism of legal closure that involves *adjudication*. The aim is to be able to settle international legal disputes concerning property and territory through international law in a binding manner. While international law provides important regulative principles for the decision-making and conduct of states in the international arena and domestically, the regulative ideal reading is insufficient to account for legal closure. This is because the regulative ideal reading of Kantian international law rests on the assumption that states will internalize the principles of international law, therefore reforming themselves internally in such a way that their conduct will reflect the norms of international law. Following Kelsen, this reading provides an account of international *ethics* rather than international *law* in a jurisprudential sense. Importantly, international rights disputes are not thereby eliminated; a state could still be wronged by another less cosmopolitically inclined state, or be involved in a *bona fide* disagreement or disputes about rights.

Without a system of legal closure, disagreements can only be solved unilaterally, that is, in a decentralized manner. At best, international rights disputes would be avoided by possibly curbing aggressive "rogue" behavior, but not legally settled when they arise. Even if we assume, for the sake of the argument, that reformed states which follow "as-if" international law are well intentioned and will follow their best judgment in international ethics, they remain in a relative state of nature in regard to each other. Individuals and groups can disagree in good faith about ethics and rights, and this is precisely the problem that necessitates a system of *external* adjudication. Characteristic of the state of nature is that due to the absence of binding external standards, individuals or states as "moral persons" are at liberty to follow their own private judgment in matters of right. Therefore, the greatest danger concerning the implementation of international law, which Kant calls our attention to, is the instrumentalization of international law as a means for advancing the political goals or even the moral views of particular states. However well-intentioned, states that attempt to use international law to advance their own moral convictions would be acting just as unilaterally as those who disguise their political agendas under the pretense of justice; both would be perpetuating the lawless international state of nature and preventing true and lasting peace. Further, this conduct would undermine the credibility and impartiality of international law and further fragment the international domain.

A possible indicator of a state's genuine commitment to international law is whether it is indeed transforming itself domestically in light of the values it preaches internationally and demands from other states; whether it is becoming domestically a stronger rule of law, capable of enforcing its laws internally, with a well-functioning, independent judiciary and consequently better integrated within the international law system. This is a standard that must be applied consistently to all states. Corradetti and Huber thus are correct to stress the role of international law in transforming states' constitutions domestically; states must be able to reform themselves towards the ideal Kantian republic, which is internally less inclined to engage in wars but also to instrumentalize international law against its genuine purpose. Nevertheless, international law cannot remain merely an "as if" to be internalized. It must constitute an increasingly centralized, external higher-order legal system with coercive powers.

6 What Kant Does Differently

I will now pause to reflect on the Kant interpretation I have developed so far. How is it different from other approaches to property rights and international law? How does it contribute to a better understanding of the relationship between an international legal order and property rights domestically? Additionally, how does my analysis advance current debates in Kant scholarship?

To answer these questions, I will contrast Kant's approach to those of some of his intellectual predecessors, John Locke and Jean-Jacques Rousseau. I will argue that Kant's account of property rights reconciles two radically opposed concepts about the nature of property rights and the function of the civil union, namely, the *natural right view* and the *conventionalist view*. The first is the view that there is a natural right to property, which renders superfluous the need for consent in the form of a social contract. On the natural right view, instituting property is a matter of social convenience; it is not needed to establish the normative basis or legitimacy of property rights. This view is illustrated by John Locke's theory of property rights. The other, diametrically opposed view, is that property is merely a matter of fact and social convention. In the absence of political institutions, individuals and groups possess what they happen to hold and can defend in the state of nature. The civil condition introduces coercive power in the defense of possessors' holdings, but also establishes the legitimacy of property rights as a purely conventional institution. This view is illustrated, somewhat inconsistently, by Jean-Jacques Rousseau. My argument is that Kant provides not only a *synthesis* of both natural right and conventionalist views, but that his version of legal positivism, which I call "non-reductive legal positivism," is the natural outcome of such a synthesis.

The natural rights view has two shortcomings from a Kantian perspective. Firstly, it relies on a theological assumption, which is incompatible with the tenets of Kant's critical philosophy. It presupposes, dogmatically, that the earth was given to us by God for the satisfaction of our needs as finite creatures. This assumption plays a fundamental role for Locke's argument. It establishes a community of land and natural resources prior to appropriation, and enables the conceptualization of acts of appropriation as *permissible*, that is, not as wronging others who are necessarily excluded from an appropriated resource. After all, the apple I pick from the tree and consume is the apple that *everybody else* will be necessarily deprived of. Kant did not dismiss religious beliefs per se, but famously argued that they have a specific place within the system of reason: they belong in the domain of faith and what we can hope for. They should be used neither as theoretical proofs nor as the normative foundation for morality or rights.[49]

Secondly, and specifically in regard to Locke's labor theory of property rights, the natural rights view fails to conceptualize rights as normative relations between persons. This is a serious problem from the perspective of *Vernunftrecht,* that is, a system of right based on pure reason. Locke's account of property conceives property rights primarily as a relation between a person (who owns herself) and an external object, which becomes something of an extension of herself due to the infusion of her labor through the act of appropriation. Her claim against others is that they should not interfere with an object insofar as what is hers, that is, her labor, *abides* in that object.[50] Locke's account thus extends self-ownership to the external world through agents' interaction with and consequent *transformation* of external things through labor. The problem is that Locke does not explain why it is the case that other agents are *obligated* to respect another person's physical possessions in the same way they should respect her physical integrity and liberty. Interfering with an object that is separate from myself is not the same as interfering with my physical integrity. Arguing that taking away the fruit of my labor constitutes theft begs the question, because it presupposes that other persons are *already* under an obligation to respect the possessions of others, without providing an account of why this is the case. Therefore, Locke does not provide a satisfactory account of the duty to respect the acquisition of others.

In contrast, the conventionalist view rejects a natural law foundation for property rights and declares them a mere human arrangement. However, as is often the case in Rousseau's writings, Rousseau's conventionalism is not without tensions and inner contradictions (see Williams 1983, pp. 82–83). As Rousseau stresses, possession in the state of nature corresponds either to the "more real" but ultimately *weak* right of the first occupant, or the effect of the *might* of the strongest in the state of nature. Rousseau seems to assume that the latter is more often the case. Although Rousseau appears to acknowledge a right of the first possessor to a previously ownerless piece of land, he soon dismisses it as a right that can be assigned "no limits" and consequently enables excessive expansion and usurpation by the strongest, as illustrated by the conquest of the Americas. He ridicules grandiose gestures such as merely "setting foot on common ground" or a "single stroke" by the Crown of

---

[49] See the "Canon of pure Reason, Second section" in the *Critique of Pure Reason*, A 804/B 832.
[50] See Locke (2003 / 1689, chapter V).

Castile as validating the acquisition of vast territories while depriving the entire human race of "what nature gives them in common." Rousseau's underlying assumption is thus that *nature* has given humanity a place of residence and the means of subsistence *in common*. Since a legitimate first possessor that has not been robbed by a stronger party is rare, all property that can be found in the state of nature is nothing other than *usurpation*. This includes the land that constitutes the territory of the kingdoms in Rousseau's time.[51] Additionally, Rousseau adopts a (mostly pessimistic) evolutionary view of human nature, according to which individuals are *transformed* through culture and civilization to develop new wants that are far removed from their genuine natural needs (McPherson 1978). This transformation of human needs through civilization also contributes to the *distortion* of natural rights. The antidote to the evils of usurpation and alienation from one's original nature is the *social contract*.

A title to property is a positive entitlement, relying on public recognition and a social contract for its existence (Rousseau 2022 / 1762, Book I, Chapter IX). Under "the powers of the City," which are much greater than those of an individual, possession acquires a public status. The state becomes the master of all the property of those subject to the social contract. However, although property is secured through the social contract, it is no more legitimate than it was before, "at least to foreigners" (Rousseau 2022 / 1762, Book I, Chapter IX). Far from robbing individual possessors in the state of nature, the social contract paradoxically turns "usurpation into true right, enjoyment into ownership" and ensures the lawful character of possession. Individual possessors are now to be regarded as the "depositaries of public property," mirroring Rousseau's assumption that nature has given its resources in common to humanity. Individuals' lawful title to property is thus established by the sovereign in a civil condition.

Rousseau's position is conventionalist because even though he accepts the idea of common possession of the earth's land and resources, what establishes the legitimacy of property rights is ultimately the social contract. Although he recognizes a minimal natural law foundation for first acts of acquisition, due to first possessors' inability to protect their acquisition, Rousseau assumes that they will have been dispossessed everywhere. This assumption seems confirmed by the radical social inequality and widespread misery prevalent in Rousseau's times. Consequently, he treats all possession in the state of nature as usurpation by the strongest as a default position. Only the social contract can

---

[51] See Rousseau (2022 / 1762, chapter IX, p. 329): "An advantage which ancient monarchs do not appear to have clearly sensed, for, calling themselves only Kings of the Persians or Scythians or Macedonians, they seem to have viewed themselves as chiefs of men rather than as owners of countries. Those of today call themselves more cleverly Kings of France, Spain, England, etc. In thus holding the land they are quite sure of holding its inhabitants."

restore the original freedom and equality of persons by *forcing them to be free* in the truest sense of the word.[52]

Although Rousseau considers property rights problematic, they must somehow be made legitimate. To become lawful, at least domestically, property rights require universality in the form of the *general will* of the people. Through the united will of all, states of affairs that were merely contingent in the state of nature acquire a public, binding character. Kant develops further Rousseau's insight that the civil condition plays a morally transformative function. Kant's approach is also distinctive in that it attempts to bridge the gap between two seemingly diametrically opposed dimensions of external relations between persons: a *real* dimension and an *ideal* dimension. While Rousseau's proposal is radical redistribution through the sovereign, Kant proposes a *mediation* between social reality and ideals of reason; his focus is on gradual reforms as opposed to revolution and a redistribution "from scratch" (Williams 1983, p. 92). Kant's approach reflects his critical philosophy: we must be aware that the ideas in question are *ideals of reason*; they express intellectual paradigms of perfection and totality that cannot be found in the world as we conceive them, and will never be fully implemented; while they have *practical* reality in guiding us to action and improving institutions, it is not only naive but also *uncritical* to attempt to implement rational ideas at any cost. Kant therefore advises us to work with the institutions and social realities we have, as opposed to violently forcing a utopia on a recalcitrant and imperfect reality.

Kant's position provides a *synthesis* of both natural law and conventionalist views. He denies that there are natural rights in the way understood by his predecessors (Williams 1983, p. 90). The Kantian synthesis is best illustrated by Kant's argument that possession in the state of nature can only be provisional (*provisorisch*), and that there is a duty to enter a civil condition, in which a system of positive laws is introduced (Kant's "Postulate of Public Right," MS 6: 307).[53] Like Rousseau, who claimed that one who does not obey the general will "can be forced to be free" (Rousseau, 2022 / 1762, Book I, Chapter VII), Kant argues that individuals can be compelled to enter a condition of public law. This is not only compatible with external freedom but indeed required by practical reason: it is a *duty* to leave the state of nature.

---

[52] There are debates about whether Rousseau is a forerunner of totalitarianism, given his ideas on social unity and the dependence of the individual upon the collective. See Nisbet (1943).

[53] It has become popular in recent Kant scholarship to discuss "provisionality" as a general concept (Hasan 2018; Messina 2019; Yeomans 2021). However, "provisional" is an attribute that applies exclusively to acquired rights in the state of nature. For my criticism of "provisionality" readings, see Pinheiro Walla (2026).

As previously discussed, the civil condition does not create property rights "from scratch," since private rights already exist in the state of nature in Kant's conception. Although possession in the state of nature enjoys the "prerogative of right" (MS 6:257), that is, has right on its side, it still lacks *necessity*, that is, the universality required to constitute a legal obligation, to impose an external duty on another person. By reconceptualizing the civil condition as the expression and instantiation of the *united will of all* (an innovation Kant adopts from Rousseau), the civil union is now able to transform the modality of provisional rights into peremptory rights. It does so by *unifying* the will of each individual right holder with all others, who then become equal and free members of the political association. The unification of individual wills under a public law system reconfigures all arrangements within the civil condition as expressions of the will of all. The legitimacy of these arrangements is thus a function of the identification of the united will with the *consent* of all members of society. Fundamental for this unification and subsequent moral transformation, however, is a condition of omnilaterality under public *positive* laws. Unfortunately, insufficient attention has been devoted in the secondary literature to the role of *positive* laws in establishing the sole adequate framework under which the modality of rights can be transformed and genuinely binding legal obligations can arise. This is the task of the next section.

7 Kant's Non-Reductive Legal Positivism: Two Concepts of Right

In this section, I examine the fundamental role of positive laws for property rights, which tends to be neglected if not altogether dismissed in the secondary literature. Although the right to acquire and use external objects is established by *Vernunftrecht*, that is, Kant's own version of natural law theory, the *legal obligation* to respect rights to external things only obtains if our external relations are structured omnilaterally, that is, if they are regulated by common external laws. This calls for the implementation of a system in which external laws are determined *publicly*; legal obligation thus requires *positive* laws. I will elucidate Kant's "non-reductive legal positivism" and explain why a *relational* reading of Kant's legal theory requires legal positivism. Finally, since presenting Kant as a legal positivist is not a widely shared position in the Kant literature, I will criticize two prominent interpretations of Kant as a non-positivist.

The requirement to enter a condition of positivity follows from Kant's Postulate of Public Right, commanding us to proceed from the state of nature into "a rightful" (*rechtlichen*) or "civil condition" (*bürgerlichen Zustand*). In the civil condition, public laws are *posited*, that is, *instituted*. Since they are promulgated by an external source (the legislator), they are also *empirical* laws. While positive laws in themselves are unable to answer the question "what is Right?" (MS 6: 229), Kant acknowledges that positive laws can nevertheless "serve as excellent guides to this" (MS 6: 230).

Although a system of laws can be just to a greater or lesser extent, it is nevertheless their *positive* character that offers the direct answer to the problem of the state of nature. The postulate of public right does not tell us that we must enter a perfectly just civil condition; it tells us to enter a civil condition *simpliciter*. Kant's legal theory reconciles the query for nonpositive principles of justice with the need to establish positive systems of law. Although positive laws do not exhaust the question of what is Right in itself, Right cannot dispense with positive laws.

One of the central tasks of a legal order is the provision and preservation of *legal certainty*. The law must be stable enough to enable those subject to it to regulate their conduct by publicly known standards, and form legitimate expectations to guide their choices, actions and plans for the future. Further, public standards that are equally binding to all are the solution to the rights disputes and disagreement about rights that are ubiquitous in the state of nature. Leaving the state of nature thus entails entering a condition regulated by *positive* laws. The positivity required by the Postulate of Public Right tends to be obscured by the view that entering the civil condition is primarily about subjecting oneself to political authority. While obedience to political authority is indeed entailed by the postulate, it is not *unmediated* subjection to a sovereign. The Kantian state is constituted by three coordinated powers: the legislative, executive and judicial authorities. As a whole, the Kantian state is the legal system itself, and does not exist independently from it. Political authority corresponds to the *executive* power of the state (MS 6: 316). Subjection to political authority is thus a function of being under a legal order or the jurisdiction of a state.

The term "legal positivism" has been applied to a number of interrelated questions and areas of inquiry, ranging from the justification of the duty to obey the law, the meta-ethical question of the possibility of moral knowledge, to theories of legal interpretation, among others (Fuesser 1996, p. 119). Legal positivism also includes a view about the nature and sources of law, including the relationship between morality and positive law. It also concerns the question of how to balance legal certainty and individuals' judgments about justice. From a Kantian perspective, the tension may appear at first as a conflict between heteronomous external norms and agents' autonomy.[54] Kant's position on the matter, however, may surprise those acquainted only with Kant's ethical works:

> One sees that in both appraisals of what is right (in terms of a right of equity and a right of necessity) the ambiguity (*aequivocatio*) arises from confusing the objective with the subjective basis of exercising the right (before reason and before a court). What someone by himself recognizes on good grounds as right will not be confirmed by a court, and what he must judge to be of itself wrong is treated with indulgence by a court; **for the concept of right, in these two cases, is not taken in the same sense.** (MS 6: 236, my emphasis)

> It is a common fault (*vitium subreptionis*) of experts on right to *misrepresent* **that rightful principle which a court is authorized and indeed bound to adopt for its own use** (hence for a subjective purpose) in order to pronounce and judge what belongs to each as his right, as if it were also **the objective principle of what is right in itself**: since the latter is very different from the former. – It is therefore of no slight importance to recognize this specific distinction and to draw attention to it. (MS 6: 297, my emphasis)[55]

The passages quoted formulate a conceptual distinction fundamental for understanding Kant's version of legal positivism: the difference between Right (*Recht*) as determined by a public system of justice, and Right as defined by reason independently of positive laws. The first has public character and is binding to those under the jurisdiction of the respective legal system; the other is private and accessible to all persons as reasoners.

In the first quoted passage, Kant explains how these two meanings of the concept of right can lead to *ambiguity* and confusion in regard to rights, as illustrated by the cases of necessity (*Notrecht*) and equity (*Billigkeit*). Kant's aim is to highlight how the verdict of a court of justice may depart from well-grounded individual judgments about rights, although it is considered *conclusively binding*.

In the second passage, Kant formulates the principles corresponding to each concept of right. One is the "rightful principle" adopted by the court of justice *for its own use* to determine what is right; the other is the objective

---

[54] Cf. MacCormick (1994), on the institutional character of the law as being "relatively heteronomous" in contrast to individual autonomy, although both law and morality are addressed to practical reason.

[55] I have slightly adapted Mary Gregor's translation to better reflect the structure of the original passage: "Es ist ein gewöhnlicher Fehler der Erschleichung (*vitium subreptionis*) der Rechtslehrer, dasjenige rechtliche Princip, was ein Gerichtshof zu seinem eigenen Behuf (also in subjektiver Absicht) anzunehmen befugt, ja sogar verbunden ist, um über jedes Einem zustehende Recht zu sprechen und zu richten, auch objektiv für das, was an sich selbst recht ist, zu halten: da das erstere doch von dem letzteren sehr unterschieden ist. – Es ist daher von nicht geringer Wichtigkeit, diese specifische Verschiedenheit kennbar und darauf aufmerksam zu machen."

principle establishing what is right *in itself*. Kant notes that "the latter is very different from the former." While the principle adopted by the court "for its own use" is linked to a "subjective purpose" of the court, right in itself is established by a principle that is objective. Therefore, additionally to the concept pairs "Right in accordance to a court of justice" and "Right in itself" we also have the corresponding distinction between "subjective" and "objective" principles of Right, tracking the idea of "external" and "internal" laws, "heteronomy" and "autonomy." Importantly, failure to understand these conceptual distinctions leads to an error of *subreption* (*Fehler der Erschleichung, vitium subreptionis*). In the first case, right as established by reason and right determined by a court of justice are mistakenly conflated; in the second, one's objective judgment about rights is considered to be the standard that the verdict of a court of justice should reflect, despite the fact that the reasoning of a court must be guided by a different "subjective" principle. Unless "right of reason" and "right according to positive laws" are clearly differentiated as two concepts of right, the concept of justice becomes ambiguous and the contribution of a positive system of laws to practical reason is obscured.

Kant can be identified as a proponent of the separation thesis of ethics and law ("law" understood here as a system of *external,* that is, *positive* laws, since the concept of law is also central to Kant's moral theory). In a minimal sense, the separation thesis consists in the claim that "determining what the law is does not necessarily, or conceptually, depend on moral or other evaluative considerations about what the law ought to be in the relevant circumstances" (Marmor 2006, p. 686). Nevertheless, Kant makes a non-positivist case for the duty to enter a condition of public laws, but also for a legal positivist understanding of the law, including a weak version of the separation thesis between law and morality. The argument is that features characteristic of external laws (positivity, omnilaterality, sources of law, the conclusive character of public justice, etc.) constitute the solution to a specific practical problem faced by persons in their external relations with each other.

Kant's version of the separation thesis is based on the insight that genuine morality is an expression of individual autonomy. Morality is something that only the agent herself can do *internally*, that is, she must *choose* to adopt rational principles of action. Therefore, it does not make sense to coerce others externally to act virtuously (MS 6: 220–1, 381–2). In contrast, positive laws pertain to the regulation of *external* actions; they are not meant to enforce morality or to control minds, since virtue is a matter of freely adopted principles rather than mere outward conduct. However, because the domain of Right (*Recht*) is itself regulated by a nonpositive, rational principle (the "Universal Principle of

Right"), the relationship between Morality and Right in Kant's theory is more complex than the dichotomy between internal and external principles of conduct.

Kant also distinguishes between legal reasoning *in the state of nature* ("private" legal reasoning) and legal reasoning by a court of justice. Because a court of justice must take into account the rules and procedure to which it is bound, it has a *public* character (call it "procedural" legal reasoning). "Private" legal reasoning does not amount to *ethical* reasoning, even though it is externally non-enforceable; it is reasoning in accordance with the pure principles of Right (*Vernunftrecht*), of which persons are capable independently from legal institutions. While Kant grants *objective* status to legal reasoning in the state of nature, he acknowledges *bindingness* in the case of the verdicts of a court of justice, although these are based on reasoning that has *subjective* status from the perspective of reason. This is because the statutes the court is bound to follow are *empirical* principles.

Identifying Kant with legal positivism may come as a shock to some readers. After all, Kant is well known for his principle-based moral theory based on the idea of autonomy of the will. How can Kant be a proponent of legal positivism, an allegedly "morally neutral" conception of law, when he stresses the unconditional character of the Categorical Imperative and the importance of thinking for oneself ? At first, legal positivism seems to contradict Kant's moral theory and hinder the realization of Kantian ideals and moral progress. Kant is often identified as an ally or a resource in defense of substantive arguments about justice; associating him with legal positivism may appear to exclude advocacy for human rights and a just society (Waldron 1996, p. 1536). Interestingly, it is precisely *because* Kant's theory relies on strong-minded agents who must think independently for themselves that legal positivism is necessary. As Waldron stresses, one's attitude about disagreement influences the way one thinks about the law. Kant's legal positivism expresses his appreciation of value pluralism and disagreement in civil society, insofar as these remain compatible with respect for public laws:

> Often the spirit of our normative arguments about justice and rights is "Here is what I would do, if I ran the country." But any discussion in jurisprudence and political philosophy must first acknowledge the fact that there are many of us and that we disagree on these matters. It is important, therefore, for theorists to pause occasionally in the elaboration and defense of their own proposals to reflect on the significance of this plurality and to grasp the point that law claims our allegiance in the circumstance of controversy over the substantive values that it embodies. That proposition can seem scary, for it invites us to compromise our heartfelt advocacy and to share our carefully

constructed intellectual world with views about justice that we regard – perhaps for good reason – as wrongheaded or iniquitous. It may help in allaying these apprehensions, however, for theorists of justice to realize that, in taking this step, they are not betraying their Kantianism; on the contrary, they are proceeding quite deliberately in the company of Immanuel Kant. (Waldron 1996, p 1537–1538)

Positive law allows us to determine the content and validity of external laws in a way that *supersedes* disagreements about rights and justice (Waldron 1996, p. 1540). This is not because disagreement is undesirable and therefore should be eliminated; on the contrary, a system of public laws *enables* diverse views to coexist by binding all persons *equally* to common public standards, without which minorities could be easily subjected to the substantive views of a majority group. This is only possible due to the omnilateral and reciprocal structure of a legal order. This formal structure enables persons to stand in a specific relation in regard to each other that affirms and safeguards their equal and free status even when the specific outcome of decision-making in accordance with positive standards does not conform to their private opinions about what would be just. I take this understanding of the role of positive laws to be not only consistent with but indeed required by a *relational* reading of Kant's legal theory, even though recent relational readings tend towards non-positivism to a greater or lesser degree.

Although proponents of the relational view such as Katrin Flikschuh recognize the role of legal institutions for the possibility of legal obligation (2010a, pp. 67–69), George Pavlakos has recently put forward a relational reading of Kant's legal theory that he describes as *radically* non-positivist. According to Pavlakos (Pavlakos 2026), the relational view stresses independence from arbitrary coercion as the fundamental feature of the Universal Principle of Right. He presents the relational view as an alternative to the "quasi-Lockean" view, according to which the Universal Principle of Right aims at promoting a self-standing notion of individual autonomy. The difference between relational and "quasi-Lockean" views lies in the relational view's emphasis on inter-personal relations, whereas the quasi-Lockean view stresses a value, namely, autonomy, that is expressed *individually* rather than relationally. Pavlakos identifies the "quasi-Lockean" reading with the "traditional" interpretation of Kant's legal philosophy, while proponents of the relational view regard themselves as offering a new interpretation.[56]

---

[56] Cf. Huber's criticism of "proto-ownership" accounts of Kant's legal theory (Huber 2022, chapter 2). Pavlakos identifies Ripstein as a proponent of the "quasi-Lockean" reading (Pavlakos 2026, p. 212, fn 40). This label is misleading and presupposes a false dichotomy, as I will criticize below.

According to Pavlakos, a "relations-first" account of law need not rely on state-bound institutions for the possibility of legal obligations. The view, he argues, is compatible with "the phenomenology of legal reasoning which does not disregard actual law-practices altogether, but reassigns them to the role of non-necessary grounds of legal obligation" (Pavlakos forthcoming, p. 206 fn 30). Therefore, while Pavlakos' radical non-positivism does not fully dispense with legal institutions, it denies their centrality to the possibility of legal obligation. All juridical demands and their public character are already provided by the Universal Principle of Right (UPR) itself.[57]

> [Radical non-positivism] points at the redundancy of state law in the context of the relational reading: why turn to law-practices to establish the interpersonal or public dimension of juridical demands if we have already established that the pre-institutional grounds of legal relations are public? (...) Freedom as independence is premised on a particular kind of interdependence from others: one obtaining when each of the interacting parties is acting with a view to the freedom of everyone else. If that's the kind of demand that is grounded by the UPR, then why appeal to an additional source of publicity? (Pavlakos 2026, p. 216)

In response, I will argue that a system of positive laws is *indispensable* as a source of publicity. This is because the Universal Principle of Right alone is insufficient to solve two specific but interrelated problems: disagreement and value pluralism, on the one hand, and the problem of legal obligation in regard to possession of external objects, on the other. This is the case even if we acknowledge that Kant's legal theory is fundamentally relational in character. Further, the distinction between the relational and "quasi-Lockean" views is misleading because both aspects, i.e. relationality and autonomy, are not only present but deeply intertwined in Kant's legal theory. From a Kantian perspective, rights can only be conceptualized as relations *between persons*; and while rights to external objects *presuppose* a juridical community – that is, persons who already stand in juridically relevant relations to each other – their mere relational aspect is not sufficient for accounting for rights to objects since they are *external* to persons themselves. Possession in the state of nature requires the introduction of a civil condition (see Section 3.2.), but it is not the only reason why legal institutions and positive laws are necessary from a Kantian perspective. Legal positivism offers the appropriate framework to deal with disagreement and value pluralism as ineradicable side effects of individual autonomy: the fact that Kantian agents must be able to "think for themselves" and the

---

[57] According to the Universal Principle of Right, "Any action is right if it can coexist with everyone's freedom in accordance with a universal law, or if on its maxim the freedom of choice of each can coexist with everyone's freedom in accordance with a universal law" (MS 6:230).

possibility of disagreement go hand in hand. Regulating external behavior by public external standards enables us to uphold the equal status of individual persons while protecting against paternalism, that is, the arbitrary interference with a person's sphere of external freedom by the state, another group, or by another individual who claims to "know best."

Kant's legal positivism is *non-reductive* because Kant accepts that there may be, if not an explicit clash, then at least an ineradicable tension between moral duty and legal obligation, as well as between private judgments about rights and the verdicts of a court of justice. Kant's legal positivism "bites the bullet" in this regard. He seeks neither to eradicate the tension between ethics and law, nor to erase the separation between the domain of private judgments about justice and legal reasoning that is bound by given statutes and procedure of a specific legal order. Despite the tensions and the "price" we may need to pay for introducing a positive system of laws that may not always lead to desired substantive results, it is nevertheless the best *Kantian* way to deal with pluralism and disagreement. Kant's legal positivism prioritizes respecting and upholding the equal status of all members of a legal order over perfectionism or "getting it right." Perfectionism in ethics or politics presupposes a substantive conception of the common good; judgments and decision making are deemed correct when they track or promote that specific conception of the common good. In contrast, a legal theory that is genuinely *relational* must focus on the *form* of external relations between persons who are equal and free. Existing legal systems are far from perfect, and some are worse than others. Even in democracies, public justice does not always match individuals' judgments about justice. So why not follow our own judgments instead? Kant's legal positivism seeks a middle-ground between the anarchist and the blind conventionalist, that is, between those who reject external laws because they do not coincide with their personal moral convictions, and those who follow positive laws dogmatically, without considering the need to reform or improve them (Hart 1958, p. 598). Moreover, the tension between law and morality preserved in Kant's legal positivism can be constructive, provided both freedom of speech and respect for the laws can be secured. The respectful criticism of the government and laws should be protected as a sacred right of the people (TP 8: 304), and can lead to legal reforms and collective enlightenment through public discourse and debate (Sweet 2024, p. 67).

However, what if the law contradicts what Kant calls "inner morality"? (MS 6: 371). So far, I have been assuming that although one may disagree with the substantive justice of a specific law or verdict of a court of justice, it is still possible to remain committed to the law. After all, tensions between a person's normative beliefs and judgments and particular laws and policies

Kant on Property Rights and International Law 59

tend to arise even in well-functioning, decent legal systems. Most people respect rules and practices they don't personally agree with, be it because they believe in the overall moral value of upholding a legal system, for convenience, out of respect for tradition, or prudential reasons, to avoid sanctions and punishment. For instance, the results of democratic elections bind both those who voted for the winning candidate and those who voted against them; disagreement with the outcome is no reason to challenge the results if there is no evidence of election fraud. We must now consider a scenario in which compliance with the law is *morally impossible* from the perspective of an agent's innermost beliefs and convictions. How would the immorality of compliance with a certain law relate to the obligation to obey that law from a Kantian perspective?

Robert Alexy identified two kinds of connections between law and morality in Kant's legal theory, both having to do with views about the consequences of moral defects for the validity of law: a *qualifying* and *classifying* connection. A qualifying connection establishes that the moral defectiveness of a law does not lead to the loss of legal validity. In contrast, a classifying connection identifies moral defectiveness with the loss of legal validity. While Kant recognizes the strictness of positivity by vehemently rejecting a right to resistance (MS 6: 320) and a right to revolution (TP 8: 299), and statements of a qualifying connection between law and morality are widespread in Kant's legal theory, Alexy argued that some claims in Kant's theory indicate the inclusion of a classifying connection between law and morality. Such statements are rare and less prominent throughout Kant's texts:

> Obey the authority over you (in whatever does not conflict with inner morality). (MS 6: 371)

For Alexy, the above quote constitutes an "exemption clause" since obedience to authority is said to be conditional upon the absence of conflict with inner morality. He also points out "nullity arguments," such as the claim that religious coercion and coercion to "unnatural sins" such as treacherous murder (*Meuchelmord*) do not belong in a civil union (Refl 19: 594–5), and the view that certain types of contracts are *null and void*, such as a contract to prevent the enlightenment of future generations (WA 8: 39) and a contract to become a serf or a slave to another (MS 6: 283). Exemption and nullity clauses suggest that legal validity may be forfeited as a result of specific (although not all) moral defects. Alexy concludes that Kant's recognition of classifying connection in his concept of law shows that he is an *inclusive non-positivist* (Alexy 2019, p. 504). According to Alexy's version of inclusive non-positivism, legal validity is lost only when an intolerable degree of injustice has been achieved. Kant's inclusive non-positivism can thus be understood in analogy with Radbruch's formula:

> The positive law, secured by legislation and power, takes precedence even when its content is unjust and fails to benefit the people, unless the conflict between statute and justice reaches such an intolerable degree that the statute, as 'flawed law', must yield to justice (Radbruch 2006 / 1946, p. 7).

I will argue that Alexy's analogy with Radbruch's formula does not reflect Kant's position. Radbruch's argument is about "degrees" of injustice: while low degrees of injustice do not invalidate law, extreme injustice forfeits its status as law. As Alexy explains, "inclusive non-positivism maintains that moral defects undermine legal validity if and only if the threshold of extreme injustice is transgressed (...). Injustice below this threshold is included in the concept of law as defective but valid law" (Alexy 2019, p. 503).

However, Kant's nullity argument does not indicate that an intolerable "degree of injustice" has been achieved, as a threshold for legal validity; instead, the nullity argument disqualifies certain practices as fit to become law *ab initio*, because they cannot become the matter of a contractual agreement between rational agents. Kant's nullity argument reflects the idea of the social contract, according to which the possibility of legal obligation ultimately rests on a conception of what rational agents could possibly consent to, that is, without *contradiction*. What constitutes contradiction depends on a conception of practical rationality. The Kantian conception is that certain rights cannot be alienated through contract if they establish the foundational conditions for legal personality, that is, our capacity to enter voluntary agreements with each other as right holders. A valid contract, that is, an agreement that creates genuine rights and corresponding obligations, presupposes these conditions, which cannot be alienated without leading to a contradiction of the practice with its own foundations. If a practice cannot be the object of *rational* consent between persons (in contrast to a purely voluntaristic, i.e., *arbitrary* agreement) it is incapable of providing the content of law under the idea of the social contract. Therefore, the requirement of non-contradiction with the rationale of the social contract *constrains* the content of the law in Kant's view from the outset, as a matter of *principle*, not of degree. It follows that Radbruch's formula does not reflect Kant's nullity argument.

Kant's exemption clause seems to fit better the analogy with Radbruch's formula. But here, too, Alexy's analogy between Kant and Radbruch is unconvincing. "Obey the authority over you (in whatever does not conflict with inner morality)" does not suggest that there is a point at which the conflict with inner morality becomes intolerable. Immorality in Kant's moral theory is not a matter of quantity, but of one's adopted principle. The *locus* of moral evaluation is always the agent's maxims or subjective principles of action. This point is illustrated by Kant's criticism of Aristotle's doctrine of the mean ("mesotes doctrine") in the *Doctrine of Virtue*:

> The distinction between virtue and vice can never be sought in the degree to which one follows certain maxims; it must rather be sought only in the specific quality of the maxims (their relation to the [moral] law). In other words, the well-known principle (Aristotle's) which locates virtue in the mean between two vices is false. Let good management, for instance, consist in the mean between two vices, prodigality and avarice: as a virtue, it cannot be represented as arising either from a gradual diminution of prodigality (by saving) or from an increase of spending on the miser's part – as if these two vices, moving in opposite directions, met in good management. **Instead, each of them has its distinctive maxim, which necessarily contradicts the maxim of the other.** (MS 6: 404, my emphasis)

Kant's exemption clause introduces a higher-order constraint on the duty to obey authority, namely the avoidance of conflict with inner morality. A conflict between two maxims arises when they are not merely logically *contrary* to each other, but *contradictory*, that is, *mutually exclusive*.[58] In that case, the morally prescribed maxim takes precedence over the other, incompatible maxim. Typically, obedience to authority and inner morality do not conflict with each other. Ethical maxims allow latitude for compliance with external laws, which are usually strict and thus have the character of perfect duties from an ethical perspective. The hierarchical relation between strict and wide obligations allows agents to reconcile the strict duty to obey the law with commitment to a variety of moral ends they have some flexibility to discharge.

There is no evidence in Kant's texts that the conflict between obedience to authority and one's inner morality would *necessarily* render public authority as such or even a specific law invalid from a legal perspective, despite the clear disqualification from the agent's *moral* standpoint. After all, the reason for not obeying authority in regard to a specific law[59] is not that it is an invalid law or no law whatsoever, but that it is an external law whose content conflicts with one's inner morality. Therefore, a classifying connection is not required for the

---

[58] Examples of merely contrary maxims in Kant's ethical theory are a maxim of reticence (disclosing little, or no more than socially expected) or of candour (disclosing more than expected by social convention). Examples of contrary maxims are truthfulness (a commitment to say only what is truthful) and a maxim of deceit for one's own convenience. See MS 6:433 fn, and Pinheiro Walla (2013).

[59] The specification "in what does not conflict with inner morality" suggests that Kant is not considering obedience to authority in general but in regard to specific matters in an ad hoc manner, when they happen to contradict inner morality.

exemption clause to obtain. As stressed by Hart, the view that one has no reason to obey an immoral law is compatible with legal positivism. Moreover, recognizing that legality is not a guarantee of justice or moral soundness is "an important and sobering political lesson we should learn from jurisprudence" (Marmor 2006, p. 692).

Even if we assumed for the sake of argument that a classifying connection obtains whenever the duty to obey authority conflicts with inner morality, that is, that the law is *always* rendered legally void when it conflicts with inner morality, we would be making a nullity argument about the law. Kant's exemption clause would thus collapse into the nullity argument. And while this would show that "not everything can be made into law"[60] according to Kant's legal theory it does not show that we should interpret Kant as defending a version of Radbruch's intolerability argument.

Another problem with Alexy's interpretation of Kant's theory as a version of Radbruch's intolerability argument is his assumption that consensus would be easier to achieve in the case of *extreme* moral defectiveness rather than "mere defectiveness" (Alexy 2019, p. 505). I am skeptical about this claim. Firstly, conscientious persons may still disagree about when an extreme degree of injustice has been achieved (Çömez 2025). Secondly, provided a significant share of the population has come to believe that annihilating a category of persons is morally justified (say, because they are demonized as a group or considered oppressors), it is questionable whether the general consensus about what constitutes extreme injustice would be informative concerning the law's moral defectiveness. The question is whether there is any intrinsic feature of extreme injustice that would lead us not only to *converge* towards its recognition but also "to get it right." For several reasons, which I will not be able to discuss here, I do believe that it is possible for groups to be *very wrong* about what they passionately believe to constitute justice or injustice.

Finally, Alexy stresses that the application of Radbruch's formula is directed to legislation *after the collapse of an unjust regime* mainly by judges and officials *in the civil condition*. This would be a retroactive application of the principle by public officials, and not primarily a principle for individual deliberation *in medias res*, as extreme injustice unfolds. If so, Alexy"s account is at odds with the claim that the position is non-positivist in the first place.

---

[60] The view that "anything can become law" is a mistaken view about the nature of legal positivism (See Raz 2007, p. 2). Kant's legal positivism also sets limits on what can become law.

8 Conclusion

In this Element, I analyzed Kant's theory of property and its relation to international law. My central claim was that underlying Kant's account of rights to external objects and territory is a more general theory of legal obligation. The possibility of legal obligation requires the establishment of a system of positive laws. But since legal obligation has a global character, it also calls for the implementation of an international legal order.

Although Kant's Universal Principle of Right is its fundamental principle, it does not exhaust the whole of Kant's legal theory. It offers a *negative* criterion for external relations, namely, the prohibition against arbitrary coercion, based on the *absence* of authority to unilaterally coerce another in the state of nature. However, it cannot account for other kinds of rights relations that require the *positive* legal capacity of right holders to bind others. It is questionable whether there would be a *duty* to leave the state of nature and implement a civil condition if there were no acquired rights in the state of nature, and the only legal duty was noninterference on the basis of innate right.[61]

The duty to leave the state of nature arises because acquired rights in the state of nature necessarily start as unilateral deeds and *yet* must impose obligations that have an omnilateral character to be genuinely binding. While it is permissible and indeed required by practical reason to divide the earth's resources, the permission to acquire does not entail the authority of the rightful possessor to unilaterally enforce her judgment about rights when her possession is contested by others. Although the rightful possessor has the "prerogative of right on her side," and this provides some normative guidance in the state of nature as to which state of affairs we should seek to preserve, unilateral coercion remains a problem from a Kantian perspective. The presumed "rightness" or "justice" of one's judgment is insufficient to bind, given its *private* character. Only omnilateral adjudication can be genuinely binding. This leads us to Kant's postulate of public right, "when you cannot avoid living side by side with all others, you ought to leave the state of nature and proceed with them into a rightful condition, that is, a condition of distributive justice" (MS 6: 307). Ultimately, only "a contract extending to the entire human race" (MS 6: 266) can provide the legal closure required for the bindingness of *rights in rem*.

Another fundamental feature of Kant's legal theory is the view that rights are *relations between persons*. I defended a relational reading of Kant's legal theory

---

[61] As Alan Brudner (2011) observes, "innate right is subject only to the imperfection inherent in the absence of a public determination and enforcement of an omnilateral obligation; it does not suffer from the problem of unilaterally imposed obligations, and so it enters the civil condition as a conclusive or valid right binding the citizen lawgiver" (p. 295).

and argued that it is not only compatible with but indeed *requires* legal positivism. I criticized non-positivist relational interpretations of Kant's legal theory, and argued that Kant offers a distinctive version of legal positivism, which I called *non-reductive legal positivism*.

Kant's non-reductive positivism is promising because it reconciles two irreducible facts about living together in a shared external world: on the one hand, the fact that we are intellectually and morally autonomous individuals capable of forming substantive views about justice, and, on the other, sincere and ineradicable disagreement about what constitutes substantive justice, as a consequence of that very intellectual and moral autonomy (cf. Waldron 1996). Far from eradicating disagreement, Kant's non-reductive legal positivism offers the best possible way to *deal* with disagreement in a way that both upholds and preserves a plurality of intellectually and morally autonomous individuals who must live with each other in a shared world.

This Element also stressed the relevance of Kant's legal theory today, given the international dimension of legal issues arising from property and territorial rights claims worldwide. The problem of legal obligation and the need for legal closure persist despite the implementation of a civil condition within isolated territories.

No territorial state on the globe can claim a historical past free of historical injustice. Most states are based on past dispossession and violence, including conquest and colonization. Kant's approach to territorial rights is *forward-looking*: its primary goal is not to restore past states of affairs to their original justice, which is impossible, but rather the gradual implementation of legal orders. Destroying an existing legal order is never permissible from a Kantian perspective, since it would mean going back into the lawless state of nature (MS 6: 320–3). Therefore, a group that upholds a legal order over a given area has a prerogative of right against groups whose aim is the destruction of that legal order. Although legal orders are always imperfect and mere approximations to the republican ideal, gradual reforms are preferable to a return to the lawless state of nature.

Abbreviations

Kant references indicate the volume and page number in the standard *Akademie Ausgabe* of Kant's *Gesammelte Schriften* (Kant 1992). Unless stated otherwise, translations are from *The Cambridge Edition of the Works of Immanuel Kant in Translation* (Kant 1992). I use the following abbreviations:

GMS = Grundlegung zur Metaphysik der Sitten / Groundwork to the metaphysics of morals (1785)

MS = Die Metaphysik der Sitten / Metaphysics of morals (1797)

R = Reflexionen / Reflections

TP = Über den Gemeinspruch: Das mag in der Theorie richtig sein, taugt aber nicht für die Praxis / On the common saying: That may be correct in theory, but it is of no use in practice (1795)

Vor-PR = Vorarbeiten zum Privatrecht / Drafts of private right

WA = Beantwortung der Frage: Was ist Aufklärung? / An answer to the question: What is enlightenment? (1784)

ZeF = Zum ewigen Frieden / Toward perpetual peace (1795)

References

Achenwall, Gottfried. 2020 (1763). *Natural Law: A Translation of the Textbook for Kant's Lectures on Legal and Political Philosophy* (Translation of Gottfried Achenwall, *Ius naturae*. 5th ed. Göttingen), edited by Pauline Kleingeld, translated by Corinna Vermeulen, with an introduction of Paul Guyer. London: Bloomsbury Academic.

Åhrén, Mattias. 2016. *Indigenous Peoples' Status in the International Legal System*. Oxford: Oxford University Press.

Alexy, Robert. 2019. "Kant's Non-Positivistic Concept of Law." *Kantian Review* 24, no. 4: 497–512.

Baiasu, Sorin. 2014. "Kant's Justification of Welfare." *Diametros* 39: 1–28.

— 2016. "Right's Complex Relation to Ethics in Kant: The Limits of Independentism." *Kant-Studien* 107, no. 1: 2–33.

Been, Vicki and Joel C. Beauvais. 2003. "The Global Fifth Amendment? NAFTA's Investment Protections and the Misguided Quest for an International 'Regulatory Takings' Doctrine." *NYU Law Review* 78, no. 30: 30–143.

Bonilla Maldonado, Daniel. 2009. "Extralegal Property, Legal Monism, and Pluralism." *University of Miami Inter-American Law Review* 40, no. 2(2): 213–238.

Brandt, Reinhard. 1982. "Das Erlaubnisgesetz, oder: Vernunft und Geschichte in Kants Rechtslehre." In *Rechtsphilosophie der Aufklärung*, edited by Reinhard Brandt, 233–285. Berlin: De Gruyter.

Brecher, Martin. 2026. "Kant on Permissive Law." In *Law and Morality in Kant*, edited by Martin Brecher and Philipp-Alexander. Cambridge: Cambridge University Press, 148–168.

Brudner, Alan. 2011. "Private Law and Kantian Right." *University of Toronto Law Journal* 61, no. 2: 279–311.

Bucher, Eugen. 2007. "Der von den Juristen verkannte apagogische Beweis – Dazu auch Kant und Kelsen." In *Festschrift für Claus-Wilhelm Canaris zum 70. Geburtstag*, edited by Andreas Heldrich, Ingo Koller, Jürgen Prölss, et al., 991–1016. München: C.H. Beck Verlag.

Byrd, B. Sharon. 2006. "The State as a 'Moral Person.'" In *Kant and Law*, 1st ed., 379–398. Routledge, 2016.

Byrd, B. Sharon and Joachim Hruschka. 2010. *Kant's Doctrine of Right: A Commentary*. Cambridge: Cambridge University Press.

2006. "The Natural Law Duty to Recognize Private Property Ownership: Kant's Theory of Property in His Doctrine of Right." *The University of Toronto Law Journal* 56, no. 2: 217–282.

Capps, Patrick and Julian Rivers. 2010. "Kant's Concept of International Law." *Legal Theory* 16, no. 4: 229–257.

Corradetti, Claudio. 2017. "Constructivism in Cosmopolitan Law: Kant's Right to Visit." *Global Constitutionalism* 6, no. 3: 412–441.

2021. *Kant, Global Politics and Cosmopolitan Law: The World Republic as a Regulative Idea of Reason*. New York: Routledge.

de Soto, Hernando. 2000. *The Mystery of Capital: Why Capitalism Triumphs in the West and Fails Everywhere Else*. New York: Basic Books.

Dagan, Hanoch. 2021. *A Liberal Theory of Property*. Cambridge: Cambridge University Press.

David Dyzenhaus. 2018. "A Monistic Approach to the Internationalization of Constitutional Law." In *New Developments in Constitutional Law: Essays in Honour of Andras Sajo*, edited by Iulia Motoc, Paulo Pinto de Albuquerque & Krzysztof Wojtyezek: 97–117. The Hague: Eleven.

Dedek, Helge. 2021. "Private Law Rights as Democratic Participation: Kelsen on Private Law and (Economic) Democracy." *University of Toronto Law Journal* 71, no. 3: 376–414.

Eberl, Oliver and Peter Niesen. 2011. *Zum ewigen Frieden: Kommentar*. Berlin: Suhrkamp Verlag.

Flikschuh, Katrin. 2010a. "Justice without Virtue." In *Kant's Metaphysics of Morals: A Critical Guide*, edited by Lara Denis: 51–70. Cambridge: Cambridge University Press.

2010b. "Kant's Sovereignty Dilemma: A Contemporary Analysis." *The Journal of Political Philosophy* 18, no. 4: 469–493.

Fuesser, Klaus. 1996. "Farewell to 'Legal Positivism': The Separation Thesis Unravelling." In *The Autonomy of Law*, edited by Robert P. George: 119–162. Oxford: Clarendon Press.

Çömez, Çağlar. 2025. "Kant's Legal Positivism and Natural Law Theory." *Kantian Review*: 1–22.

Guyer, Paul. 2002. "Kant's Deductions of the Principles of Right." In *Kant's Metaphysics of Morals: Interpretive Essays*, edited by Mark Timmons: 23–64. Oxford: Oxford University Press.

2024. *The Moral Foundation of Right*. Elements in the Philosophy of Immanuel Kant. Cambridge, England: Cambridge University Press.

Hruschka Joachim. 2004. "The Permissive Law of Practical Reason in Kant's "Metaphysics of Morals. Law and Philosophy, 23(1), 45–72. http://www.jstor.org/stable/4150563

Hart, Herbert Lionel Adolphus. 2012 (1961). *The Concept of Law.* 3rd ed., edited by Leslie Green, Joseph Raz and Penelope A. Bulloch. Oxford: Clarendon Press.

1958. "Positivism and the Separation of Law and Morals." *Harvard Law Review* 71, no. 4: 593–629.

Hasan, Rafeeq. 2018. "The Provisionality of Property Rights in Kant's Doctrine of Right," *Canadian Journal of Philosophy* 48: 850–876.

Hobbes, Thomas. 1964 (1642). *De Cive or the Citizen.* Edited by Sterling P Lamprecht. New York: Appleton-Century-Crofts.

Höffe, Ottfried. 2006. *Kant's Cosmopolitan Theory of Law and Peace.* Cambridge: Cambridge University Press.

Hohfeld, Wesley Newcomb. 1917. "Fundamental Legal Conceptions as Applied in Judicial Reasoning." *The Yale Law Journal* 26: 710–70.

Holtman, Sarah Williams. 2018 *Kant on Civil Society and Welfare.* Cambridge: Cambridge University Press.

Horn, Christoph. 2014. *Nichtideale Normativität: Ein neuer Blick auf Kants politische Philosophie.* Berlin: Suhrkamp Verlag.

2004. "The Permissive Law of Practical Reason in Kant's Metaphysics of Morals." *Law and Philosophy* 23: 45–72.

Huber, Jakob. 2022. *Kant's Grounded Cosmopolitanism: Original Common Possession and the Right to Visit.* Oxford: Oxford University Press.

Jakab, András. 2004. "Kelsen's Doctrine of International Law: Between Epistemology and Politics." *Austrian Review of International and European Law* (ARIEL), 9(1): 49–62.

Kant, Immanuel. 1992. *The Cambridge Edition of the Works of Immanuel Kant in Translation.* General editors Paul Guyer and Allen W. Wood. Cambridge: Cambridge University Press.

1902. *Gesammelte Schriften.* Herausgegeben von der Deutschen Akademie der Wissenschaften. Berlin: De Gruyter.

Kelsen, Hans. 1997 (1934). *Introduction to the Problems of Legal Theory: A Translation of the First Edition of the Reine Rechtslehre or Pure Theory of Law.* Translated by Bonnie Litschewski Paulson and Stanley L. Paulson. Oxford: Clarendon Press.

1967 (1960). *Pure Theory of Law.* Translated from *Reine Rechtslehre* (2nd revised ed.) by Max Knight. Berkeley: University of California Press

Kennedy, Christina M., Brandie Fariss, James R. Oakleaf et al. 2023. "Indigenous Peoples' Lands are Threatened by Industrial Development; Conversion Risk Assessment Reveals Need to Support Indigenous Stewardship." *One Earth* 6, no. 8: 1032–1049.

Kleingeld, Pauline. 2012. *Kant and Cosmopolitanism*. Cambridge: Cambridge University Press.

2004. "Approaching Perpetual Peace: Kant's Defence of a League of States and His Ideal of a World Federation." *European Journal of Philosophy* 12: 304–325.

Koskenniemi, Martti. 2007. "Constitutionalism as Mindset: Reflections on Kantian Themes about International Law and Globalization." *Theoretical Inquiries in Law* 8, no. 1: 9–36.

Kriebaum, Ursula and August Reinisch. 2019. "Property, Right to, International Protection." In *Max Planck Encyclopedia of Public International Law*, edited by Anne Peters: 522–533. Oxford: Oxford University Press.

Kumm, Mattias. 2013. "The Cosmopolitan Turn in Constitutionalism: An Integrated Conception of Public Law." *Indiana Journal of Legal Studies* 20: 605–628.

Lauterpacht, Hersch. 1977 (1945). "Sovereignty and Federation in International Law." In *International Law: Being the Collected Papers of Hersch Lauterpacht, Volume 3 The Law of Peace Parts II-VI*, edited by Elihu Lauterpacht: 5–28. Cambridge: Cambridge University Press.

Lawson-Remer, Terra. 2012. "The Paradox of Property Rights and Economic Development." *Council on Foreign Relations*, November 12. www.cfr.org/blog/paradox-property-rights-and-economic-development (Accessed July 29, 2024).

Leben, Charles. 1998. "Hans Kelsen and the Advancement of International Law." *European Journal of International Law* 9: 287–305.

Locke, John. 2003 (1689). "Second Treatise of Government." In *Two Treatises of Government and a Letter Concerning Toleration*, edited by Ian Shapiro: 100–209. New Haven: Yale University Press.

Loriaux, Sylvie. 2020. *Kant and Global Distributive Justice*. Cambridge: Cambridge University Press.

Lukashuk, Igor I. 1989. "The Principle *Pacta Sunt Servanda* and the Nature of Obligation Under International Law." *The American Journal of International Law* 83, no. 3: 513–518.

MacCormick, Neil. 1994. "The Concept of Law and 'The Concept of Law.'" *Oxford Journal of Legal Studies* 14, no. 1: 1–23.

Marmor, Andrei. 2006. "Legal Positivism: Still Descriptive and Morally Neutral." *Oxford Journal of Legal Studies* 26: 683–704.

Marx, Karl, and Friedrich Engels. 1963 (1848). *The Communist Manifesto of Karl Marx and Friedrich Engels*. Edited by D. B. Riazanov. New York: Russell & Russell.

McPherson, Crawford Brough. (ed.). 1978. *Property: Mainstream and Critical Positions*. Toronto: University of Toronto Press.

Messina, James P. 2019. "Kant's Provisionality Thesis." *Kantian Review* 24: 439–463.

Nisbet, Robert A. 1943. "Rousseau and Totalitarianism." *The Journal of Politics* 5, no. 2: 93–114.

Pavlakos, George. 2026. "The Kantian Legal Relation as Radical Non-positivism." In *Law and Morality in Kant*, edited by Martin Brecher and Philipp Hirsch. Cambridge: Cambridge University Press, 195–219.

Pinheiro Walla, Alice. 2024. "Property Rights and the International Law System." In *The Palgrave Handbook of International Political Theory Volume II*, edited by Howard Williams, David Boucher, Peter Sutch, David Reidy, and Alexandros Koutsoukis: 209–228. Cham: Palgrave Macmillan.

2022. "Honeste Vive: Dignity in Kant's Rechtslehre." In *Human Dignity and the Kingdom of Ends: Kantian Perspectives and Practical Applications*, edited by Adam Cureton and Jan-Willem van der Rijt: 109–131. New York: Routledge.

2020a. "Kant and Climate Change: A Territorial Rights Approach." In *Moral Theory and Climate Change: Ethical Perspectives on a Warming Planet*, edited by Ben Eggleston and Dale E. Miller: 99–115. New York: Routledge.

2020b. "Private Property and Territorial Rights: A Kantian Alternative to Contemporary Debates." In *Reason, Normativity and Law: New Essays in Kantian Philosophy*. Alice Pinheiro Walla, Mehmet Ruhi Demiray (Eds.) Cardiff: University of Wales Press, 213–232.

2019. "A Kantian Foundation for Welfare Rights." *Jurisprudence* 11, no. 1: 76–91.

2026. "Bridging the Juridical Gap: Ethical and Juridical Duties in the Absence of Political Institutions." In *Law and Morality in Kant*, edited by Martin Brecher and Philipp Hirsch. Cambridge: Cambridge University Press, 169–191.

2017. "Global Government or Global Governance? Realism and Idealism in Kant's Legal Theory." *Journal of Global Ethics* 13, no. 3: 312–25.

2014. "Human Nature and the Right to Coerce in Kant's Doctrine of Right." *Archiv für Geschichte der Philosophie* 96, no. 1: 126–139.

2013. "Virtue and Prudence in a Footnote of the Metaphysics of Morals (MS VI: 433n)." *Jahrbuch für Recht und Ethik* 21: 307–323.

Radbruch, Gustav. 2006 (1946). "Statutory Lawlessness and Supra-Statutory Law." Translated by Bonnie Litschewski Paulson and Stanley L. Paulson. *Oxford Journal of Legal Studies* 26, no. 1: 1–11.

Raz, Joseph. 2007. "The Argument from Justice, or How Not to Reply to Legal Positivism." In *Law, Rights and Discourse. The Legal Philosophy of Robert Alexy*, edited by George Pavlakos: 17–36. Oxford: Hart.

Ripstein, Arthur. 2021. *Kant and the Law of War*. Oxford: Oxford University Press.

Rousseau, Jean-Jaques. 2022 (1762). "Of the Social Contract." In *Political Philosophy: The Essential Texts*, 4th ed., edited by Steven M. Cahn: Oxford: Oxford University Press, 323–348.

— 2019. "Political Independence, Territorial Integrity and Private Law Analogies." *Kantian Review* 24, no. 4: 573–604.

— 2009. *Force and Freedom: Kant's Legal and Political Philosophy*. Cambridge: Harvard University Press.

Rühl, Ulli F. H. 2010. "Der intelligible Besitz – und nicht Eigentum – als rechtsmetaphysischer Fundamentalbegriff in Kants ‚Privatrecht.'" *Jahrbuch für Recht und Ethik / Annual Review of Law and Ethics* 18: 563–80.

Sprankling, John G. 2012. "The Emergence of International Property Law." *North Carolina Law Review* 90, no. 2: 461–509.

Sweet, Kristi. 2024. "Kant on Free Speech: Criticism, Enlightenment, and the Exercise of Judgement in the Public Sphere." *Kantian Review* 29, no. 1: 61–80.

Tierney, Brian. 2001a. "Kant on Property: The Problem of the Permissive Law." *Journal of the History of Ideas* 62: 301–312.

— 2001b. "Permissive Natural Law and Property: Gratian to Kant." *Journal of the History of Ideas* 62: 381–399.

von Daniels, Detlef. 2019. "Kant and Kelsen on International Law." In *Natur und Freiheit: Akten des XII. Internationalen Kant-Kongresses*, edited by Violetta L. Waibel, Margit Ruffing and David Wagner: 2623–2632. Berlin: De Gruyter.

Waldron, Jeremy. 1996. "Kant's Legal Positivism." *Harvard Law Review* 109, no. 7: 1535–1566.

Weinrib, Jacob. 2008. "The Juridical Significance of Kant's 'Supposed Right to Lie.'" *Kantian Review* 13, no. 1: 141–170.

Willaschek, Marcus. 1997. "Why the Doctrine of Right Does Not Belong in the Metaphysics of Morals: On Some Basic Distinctions in Kant's Moral Philosophy." *Jahrbuch für Recht und Ethik* 5: 471–476.

Williams, Howard. 1983. *Kant's Political Philosophy*. New York: St. Martin's Press.

— 2001. "Metamorphosis or Palingenesis? Political Change in Kant." *The Review of Politics* 63, no. 4: 693–722.

Yeomans, Christopher. 2021. "Kant and the Provisionality of Property." In *Kant on Morality, Humanity, and Legality: Practical Dimensions of Normativity*, edited by Ansgar Lyssy and Christopher Yeomans: 253–277. Cham: Palgrave Macmillan.

Ypi, Lea. 2014. "A Permissive Theory of Territory Rights." *European Journal of Philosophy* 22, no. 2: 288–312.

2010. "Natura Daedala Rerum? On the Justification of Historical Progress in Kant's Guarantee of Perpetual Peace." *Kantian Review* 14, no. 2: 118–148.

Acknowledgments

Earlier versions of the ideas developed in this Element were presented at the Philosophy Departments at the University of Toronto, McMaster University, the University of Caxias do Sul, and at the International Relations Department of the Hebrew University of Jerusalem. I would like to thank Navya Sheth, Mitchell Tam, and Logan Ginther for their invaluable research support; Howard Williams, Stefan Sciaraffa, and two anonymous referees for helpful suggestions and constructive criticism which greatly helped me improve this Element. This research was possible thanks to an Insight Grant of the Canadian Social Sciences and Humanities Research Council (SSHRC).

For Trevor Levine, for sustaining Kant scholarship with love, porridge and good coffee.

Cambridge Elements

The Philosophy of Immanuel Kant

Desmond Hogan
Princeton University

Desmond Hogan joined the philosophy department at Princeton in 2004. His interests include Kant, Leibniz and German rationalism, early modern philosophy, and questions about causation and freedom. Recent work includes 'Kant on the Foreknowledge of Contingent Truths', *Res Philosophica* 91(1) (2014); 'Kant's Theory of Divine and Secondary Causation', in Brandon Look (ed.) *Leibniz and Kant*, Oxford University Press (2021); 'Kant and the Character of Mathematical Inference', in Carl Posy and Ofra Rechter (eds.) *Kant's Philosophy of Mathematics Vol. I*, Cambridge University Press (2020).

Howard Williams
University of Cardiff

Howard Williams was appointed Honorary Distinguished Professor at the Department of Politics and International Relations, University of Cardiff in 2014. He is also Emeritus Professor in Political Theory at the Department of International Politics, Aberystwyth University, a member of the Coleg Cymraeg Cenedlaethol (Welsh-language national college) and a Fellow of the Learned Society of Wales. He is the author of *Marx* (1980); *Kant's Political Philosophy* (1983); *Concepts of Ideology* (1988); *Hegel, Heraclitus and Marx's Dialectic* (1989); *International Relations in Political Theory* (1992); *International Relations and the Limits of Political Theory* (1996); *Kant's Critique of Hobbes: Sovereignty and Cosmopolitanism* (2003); *Kant and the End of War* (2012) and is currently editor of the journal Kantian Review. He is writing a book on the Kantian legacy in political philosophy for a new series edited by Paul Guyer.

Allen Wood
Indiana University

Allen Wood is Ward W. and Priscilla B. Woods Professor Emeritus at Stanford University. He was a John S. Guggenheim Fellow at the Free University in Berlin, a National Endowment for the Humanities Fellow at the University of Bonn and Isaiah Berlin Visiting Professor at the University of Oxford. He is on the editorial board of eight philosophy journals, five book series and The Stanford Encyclopedia of Philosophy. Along with Paul Guyer, Professor Wood is co-editor of The Cambridge Edition of the Works of Immanuel Kant and translator of the Critique of Pure Reason. He is the author or editor of a number of other works, mainly on Kant, Hegel and Karl Marx. His most recently published books are *Fichte's Ethical Thought*, Oxford University Press (2016) and *Kant and Religion*, Cambridge University Press (2020). Wood is a member of the American Academy of Arts and Sciences.

About the Series

This Cambridge Elements series provides an extensive overview of Kant's philosophy and its impact upon philosophy and philosophers. Distinguished Kant specialists provide an up-to-date summary of the results of current research in their fields and give their own take on what they believe are the most significant debates influencing research, drawing original conclusions.

Cambridge Elements⁼

The Philosophy of Immanuel Kant

Elements in the Series

The Moral Foundation of Right
Paul Guyer

The Postulate of Public Right
Patrick Capps and Julian Rivers

Kant on the History and Development of Practical Reason
Olga Lenczewska

Kant's Ideas of Reason
Katharina T. Kraus

Kant on Marriage
Charlotte Sabourin

Kant and Teleology
Thomas Teufel

Kant on Social Suffering
Nuria Sánchez Madrid

Kant's Natural Philosophy
Marius Stan

Kant Incorporated
Garrath Williams

Kant on Respect (Achtung)
Jörg Noller

Kant on Citizenship and Poverty
Nicholas Vrousalis

Kant on Property Rights and International Law
Alice Pinheiro Walla

A full series listing is available at: www.cambridge.org/EPIK

For EU product safety concerns, contact us at Calle de José Abascal, 56–1°,
28003 Madrid, Spain or eugpsr@cambridge.org.

www.ingramcontent.com/pod-product-compliance
Lightning Source LLC
LaVergne TN
LVHW011854060526
838200LV00054B/4335